"Steve Elliott has a beautiful ability to use words to weave timeless truths into our ordinary lives. As he unpacks the story of Joseph you will find your heart leaning in to seize the practical principles that unfold and welcome them into your own context. Real transformation is a real possibility."

Dr. Daniel P B. Lewis
Th⌐ ⌐ ⌐ndation

"Steve Elliott writes with a n⌐ ⌐oice. In *Joseph: A Story About* ⌐ into the center of what forgiv⌐ ⌐ ⌐amily tangled and torn by betra⌐ ⌐nd deceit of many kinds. While Elliott br⌐ ⌐ghts into the story, his best strength may be that ⌐ a thoughtful and contemplative writer who leaves you with lots to think about and reflect upon."

Dr. David Rambo
former President of the Christian
and Missionary Alliance

"Steve Elliot is a communicator worthy of your attention. He has mine."

Dr. John Stumbo
President of the Christian and
Missionary Alliance

"God is in the business of redeeming families, not just individuals. In this engaging and insightful book, Steve Elliott artfully unfolds the biblical story of Joseph, revealing how God works not only to transform Joseph, but also the broken, dysfunctional, patriarchal family of which he is a part. Here the Scripture is practically applied to family relationships, systems, and dynamics. The result is biblical exposition at its best. And if God could change Joseph's family, then surely, through His wisdom, grace, and power, He can change ours, too!"

Dr. Stephen A. Seamands
Professor of Christian Doctrine
Asbury Theological Seminary

JOSEPH

A Story About a Family

STEPHEN V. ELLIOTT

 Seedbed

Unless otherwise noted, Scripture quotations are taken from THE HOLY BIBLE, NEW INTERNATIONAL VERSION®, NIV® Copyright © 1973, 1978, 1984, 2011 by Biblica, Inc.™ Used by permission. All rights reserved worldwide.

Scripture quotations marked NLT are taken from the Holy Bible, New Living Translation, copyright 1996, 2004. Used by permission of Tyndale House Publishers, Inc., Wheaton, Illinois 60189. All rights reserved.

Scripture quotations marked NASB are taken from the New American Standard Bible®. Copyright © 1960, 1962, 1968, 1971, 1972, 1973, 1975, 1977, 1995 by The Lockman Foundation. Used by permission.

Scripture quotations marked NRSV are taken from the Holy Bible: New Revised Standard Version/Division of Christian Education of the National Council of Churches of Christ in the United States of America. Used by permission. All rights reserved.

Scripture quotations marked RSV are taken from the Revised Standard Version of the Bible, copyright 1952 [2nd edition, 1971] by the Division of Christian Education of the National Council of the Churches of Christ in the United States of America. Used by permission. All rights reserved.

Scripture quotations marked KJV are taken from the Holy Bible, King James Version, Cambridge, 1796.

Printed in the United States of America

Cover illustration and design by Nikabrik Design
Page design by PerfecType, Nashville, Tennessee

Elliott, Stephen V.
  Joseph : a story about a family / Stephen V. Elliott. – Frankin, Tennessee : Seedbed Publishing, ©2016.

  xiv, 170 ; 22 cm.

  Includes bibliographical references (pages 169-170).
  ISBN 9781628242232 (paperback : alk. paper)
  ISBN 9781628242249 (Mobi)
  ISBN 9781628242256 (ePub)
  ISBN 9781628242263 (uPDF)

  1. Joseph (Son of Jacob). 2. Bible. Genesis, XXXVII-XLIV -- Commentaries. 3. Families -- Biblical teaching. 4. Interpersonal relations – Biblical teaching. I. Title.

BS580.J6 E4 2016   222/.1106   2016930979

SEEDBED PUBLISHING
Franklin, Tennessee
seedbed.com

to my Marilyn
. . . Always.

Contents

Acknowledgments

THE LATE VANCE Havner, quoting a fellow evangelist, once wrote, "When I started out preaching, I said I'd be original or nothing. I soon found out that I was both!"

When we are most honest, we all must acknowledge that we stand on someone else's shoulders. And I stand on many. I am grateful to the women and men who have dedicated their lives to the thoughtful academic study and pastoral efforts that have shaped my work with insights I cannot claim as original, but which have found their way into my heart and life and taken root in how I believe and think . . . how I work and write. So thank you.

I am grateful for the people of the church I love, First Alliance Church in Lexington, Kentucky, for their encouragement to write what they were first to hear on Sundays that now seem so long ago. I offer my sincere and honest thanks to my whole staff, but especially to Amy Davis, who did so much editing and formatting trying to make me look good in print.

And to the good folks at Seedbed Publishing. Holly Jones, take a bow . . . for keeping me in line and on time and preventing me from self-publishing a mistake-filled disaster. You all are real good folks.

Introduction

HOME IS WHERE the story begins for each of us. Your story and mine find their roots, their DNA, in the place where it began for all of us . . . at home. The stamp of life was placed on us there. All we are today traces its way back to our parents and siblings, our contexts and circumstances, our sorrows and pains, our joys and discoveries. Home really is where our story begins. And Joseph, the subject of this book, had a home.

I commonly say that all the great truths of the Bible are about relationships: ours with God and ours with one another. Everything else in Scripture is valuable but not as central. The relationship we have with God on a vertical plane is meant to empower and bring life to the relationships we have on a horizontal plane with everyone else. Essentially, all of life revolves around those two sets of relationships.

When those relationships are fractured and splintered or badly bent and twisted out of shape, life as it was meant to be lived just doesn't work. And for most of us, that's most days. For the rest of you folks, who have life perfectly constructed, you can stop reading and pray for the rest of us.

None of us, it seems, get to live some kind of conflict-free, Christian-theme-park life. We live in the real world, where real life offers a lot of days when life just simply doesn't work. And it doesn't work because our relationships are bruised or broken. Vertically or horizontally. Such is real life, and it's not for the faint of heart.

And that is why real life calls for real Christianity. Not the plastic, "take these two Bible verses and call me in the morning" kind of answer. Not the "ask your pastor if this truth is right for you" kind of response. Just the real stuff of biblical truth for the real stuff of life.

On a day when life unfolds as it should, it doesn't ask us for very much biblical faith, does it? Life doesn't ask for vigorous trust in God when all is right with the world. When your primary relationships are all in order, you can handle most of what unfolds in a day.

> All the great truths of the Bible are about relationships: ours with God and ours with one another.

But such days in my world are rare. And I'm guessing they are rare for you as well. What we seem to get on most days is real life, the broken kind, the kind that doesn't work right, the days you endure and just try to live through. And that life can eat your lunch. Put enough of those days together and something in your soul just dies.

When too many of your days are littered with conflict and disappointment, betrayals great and small, promises broken or forgotten, you need more than glib, clichéd, Sunday school answers. You need all that God can be for you when your ex calls or when the kids throw your failures in your face, when real life kicks in and traffics in all of its usual defeat and discouragement.

And on most of those days, you find what Joseph found: the stuff of real life is family stuff. All he contended with over the course of his life found its way back home. Back to the home where his story began. Back to his family.

But you know that. Because you have a family. Your spouse or your kids, your in-laws or your siblings are in the middle of it. If it's not them, it's the parents who long ago lost any sense of boundaries, who interfere and throw hand grenades into your world.

It's all right there in your family, isn't it? You can be single and choking on your loneliness or married and discovering that life can still feel as empty as a vacant house; the family stuff is always there. On a lot of days, you can feel like Joseph looking up from a dried-up cistern on the back side of a desert, wondering what you did to deserve this.

It doesn't matter where you are in your journey: the stuff of real life, the family stuff, is always right in your face. You are always contending with it.

And all the relational work it takes to make real life work takes its toll. You see it looking back at you every morning in the mirror. Every crease, every wrinkle, every worry line . . . your face is your journey's map. Your family charted most of it. Your bleary eyes are the lamp by which you read it. And it's not pretty, and nothing from Revlon or Oil of Olay can fix it.

> Real life calls for real Christianity.

A friend once told me of a time when a group of Western missionaries were gathered with a group of national African pastors for a spiritual renewal retreat. The guest speaker told them he was going to speak on Joseph and asked them in a breakout session what they thought the story of Joseph was all about. In summary, all the Western missionaries said it was a story about redemption. But all the African pastors said it was a story about a family.

It is in this sense of the African view of the story that I come to this study in the life of Joseph. I look at his life through the lens of his relationships with his family. In these chapters, I have tried to unfold what it meant for him to do the hard work of real life, even as I continue to process my discoveries from his life through the life of my own family's story.

In Joseph's story we discover that God is findable in the midst of the real stuff of life, the relationships that shape and misshape everyday life. And yes, God does work redemptively in the midst of it. But when all is said and done, Joseph's story is a story about a family. Maybe even your family.

Negatives Found in the Family Album

✦ Genesis 37:1–20 ✦

Someone told [Jesus], "Your mother and brothers are standing outside, wanting to speak to you." He replied to him, "Who is my mother, and who are my brothers?" Pointing to his disciples, he said, "Here are my mother and my brothers."

—Matthew 12:47–49

Friends are God's apology for family.

—Fred Smith

AS A KID growing up, did you ever think that you were the only normal one in your family? Of course you did. We all did. And for those of us who are now grown, doesn't the current behavior of the rest of our family confirm our childhood suspicions?

I know for sure that I'm the only one who is normal in my family. Aren't you sure? I mean, the others are all nuts, right? As the tired old saying goes, normal in our house was just a setting on the dryer. But I'm pretty sure I must have been adopted or left on their doorstep in a basket. Haven't you ever had that haunting sense that you don't belong in your family picture?

Unlike most pastors, I come from a long line of sinners. If dysfunction were a color, my family origin would be a rainbow. And when I became a Christian as an adult, things went from bad to worse.

If you've been around the church awhile, you've probably noticed a phenomenon: forgiven people, through no effort of their own, have this way of making unforgiven people feel guiltier. The early fractures of shame and guilt in my family foundation made for Grand Canyon–sized separations later that remain unprocessed and unaddressed to this day. My family album is kept in a drawer for a reason.

> If dysfunction were a color, my family origin would be a rainbow.

Is that where you keep yours? Don't be alarmed. Next time you're at the mall, take notice of the photographer's kiosk in the hallway or in some hole-in-the-wall location. You'll see idyllic pictures of idyllic families: everyone in white shirts and blue jeans, on the grass under a tree, blue sky, sunshine, smiles imported from a smile factory in sunny Florida. Even the family pets are smiling.

And as you look at that airbrushed picture of perfection, you just know what the teenage kid in the picture is thinking: *If my friends see this, I'll die! How did I end up with this bunch? What is it with my family?! Get me outta this picture!* Which is another way of coming at the truth: a picture may be worth a thousand words, but it seldom tells the whole story. Family pictures hanging on the wall at home or sitting on a desk at the office don't capture all the complexities of family life. It's just not possible. And some of those pictures are just pain in a frame.

Like the one that hung on the goat-skinned wall in the tent of a guy named Jacob. The chapters running up to Genesis 37 give us the family story behind the family portrait of Jacob, the son of Isaac, son of Abraham. Three generations in for the people of God and normal family life was anything but normal. And the first twenty verses of Genesis 37 begin to tell us what abnormal looks like.

Jacob lived in the land where his father had stayed, the land of Canaan. This is the account of Jacob's family line.

Joseph, a young man of seventeen, was tending the flocks with his brothers, the sons of Bilhah and the sons of Zilpah, his father's wives, and he brought their father a bad report about them.

Now Israel loved Joseph more than any of his other sons, because he had been born to him in his old age; and he made an ornate robe for him. When his brothers saw that their father loved him more than any of them, they hated him and could not speak a kind word to him.

Joseph had a dream, and when he told it to his brothers, they hated him all the more. He said to them, "Listen to this dream I had: We were binding sheaves of grain out in the field when suddenly my sheaf rose and stood upright, while your sheaves gathered around mine and bowed down to it."

Some of those pictures are just pain in a frame.

His brothers said to him, "Do you intend to reign over us? Will you actually rule us?" And they hated him all the more because of his dream and what he had said.

Then he had another dream, and he told it to his brothers. "Listen," he said, "I had another dream, and this time the sun and moon and eleven stars were bowing down to me."

When he told his father as well as his brothers, his father rebuked him and said, "What is this dream you had? Will your mother and I and your brothers actually come and bow down to the ground before you?" His brothers were jealous of him, but his father kept the matter in mind.

Now his brothers had gone to graze their father's flocks near Shechem, and Israel said to Joseph, "As you know, your brothers are grazing the flocks near Shechem. Come, I am going to send you to them."

"Very well," he replied.

So he said to him, "Go and see if all is well with your brothers and with the flocks, and bring word back to me." Then he sent him off from the Valley of Hebron.

When Joseph arrived at Shechem, a man found him wandering around in the fields and asked him, "What are you looking for?"

He replied, "I'm looking for my brothers. Can you tell me where they are grazing their flocks?"

"They have moved on from here," the man answered. "I heard them say, 'Let's go to Dothan.'"

So Joseph went after his brothers and found them near Dothan. But they saw him in the distance, and before he reached them, they plotted to kill him.

"Here comes that dreamer!" they said to each other. "Come now, let's kill him and throw him into one of these cisterns and say that a ferocious animal devoured him. Then we'll see what comes of his dreams." (Gen. 37:1–20)

One of the things I like about the Bible is its integrity in how it presents people. If the Bible is out to impress us with the sterling quality of the people who followed God, it could use some editorial help. Because these people aren't that sterling.

Perhaps that is why in her book *The Preaching Life*, Barbara Brown Taylor wrote, "My relationship with the Bible is not a romance but a marriage, and one I am willing to work on in all the usual ways: by living with the text day in and day out, by listening to it and talking back to it . . . *by refusing to distance myself from the parts of it I do not like or understand.*"[1]

We might want a more sanitized version of Scripture, but apparently we got the one God wanted us to have: one that is full of real humanity. There are no plastic, dashboard saints in Scripture, just real people with flaws and foibles that God, nevertheless, used for His honor and glory. Which, for me, being flawed as I am, is comforting news. But for you of course, it's not an issue at all. Ahem.

In Genesis 37 we meet some of Jacob's family, and the family portrait is not airbrushed. There's a story behind the photograph that hung on the wall of that goat-skinned tent. And that story shapes the account contained in the first twenty verses, just as your own family's history affects and shapes the current dynamics of your present family's life.

> There are no plastic, dashboard saints in Scripture, just real people with flaws and foibles.

In that eight-by-ten glossy, you see Jacob, there in the middle, the father of that brood. Jacob's name means "deceiver" or "usurper" or my personal favorite paraphrase, "little cheat." He came by this dishonest name honestly. Jacob stole his older brother's inheritance by deception and lived most of his adult life estranged from his father, mother, and only brother. Not a good starting point for building a wholesome, strong family identity, was it?

Then there was Leah, his first wife. He got Leah in exchange for seven years of hard labor for her father, Laban. Only he had worked to get the other daughter, the pretty one, Rachel. But when the time came, in an irony hard to miss, her old man cheated the little cheat and gave him Leah, the older daughter, the one Jacob never really did love.

Now, don't hurry past that thought. Pause and take a breath. Breathe the thought of it in. In all his life with her, Jacob never really loved Leah. Think about that for a moment and what that would mean for life in Jacob's family. When choices were being made. When money was being spent. When the lights were turned out for the night. What must "unloved" have looked like in the daily-ness of life?

> Where the earth quakes, cracks form in the foundation of family life. And what falls through those cracks is family life itself, as it was meant to be known.

I've always thought that Proverbs 30:21–23 could break anyone's heart if we'd let it speak honestly, let it fall with its full weight: "Under three things the earth quakes, and under four, it cannot bear up . . ." And the third one is? "An unloved woman when she gets a husband" (NASB).

"Under three things the earth quakes . . ." And where the earth quakes, cracks form in the foundation of family life. And what falls through those cracks is family life itself, as it was meant to be known. What a heavy, heavy emptiness Leah must have experienced in Jacob's home. But some of you who read these words know of it firsthand, don't you?

Jacob and Leah married and had six boys and one daughter together. But that didn't stop Jacob from marrying Rachel as well. She was, after all, the pretty one . . . the kind who gets a solo shot at the photo kiosk in the mall. She's what family albums are kept for . . . and you hope any girls in the family get their looks from her side of the gene pool.

And here in the startling honesty of Scripture is where you need to sort out what the Bible *records* from what the Bible *teaches*. The Bible teaches that polygamy is wrong. It's sin. The whole weight of the Bible's teaching on marriage is one man, one woman, in an exclusive covenant relationship until death.

And the Bible records what Jacob did, not simply what he should have done. The Bible does not hide his sin in order that we might be fooled into thinking he was a spiritual superstar . . . some two-dimensional flannelgraph figure from a Sunday school class. But the Bible also doesn't hide how that very sin crippled all the relationships within the wider family, in some respects, for many, many generations to follow.

When you grow up, you figure some things out. Like how my mother trapped my father into marrying her, into doing "the honorable thing." It was never spoken of in our home. Ever. But when thirty years go by without ever knowing or celebrating a wedding anniversary, you know that something is wrong.

And it was. I figured out later that my older brother's birthday came too soon after the wedding date. And the guilt of that meant you couldn't celebrate life as it was meant to be celebrated: you had to hide it in a corner of shame. And that shame gets compounded by every other noncelebration of marital life in the home: the absence of intimacy, of wholesome affection . . . of love meant to be spoken of that goes entirely unspoken.

That is the nature of secrets. *Secrets have power, and it's a power to deform.* While the truth sets you free and forms you in ways that serve your wellness and wholeness, secrets tie you in knots and issue only brokenness. In family life, secrets prove poisonous.

Over time, the secrets in my family produced a crippling shame that completely deformed and disfigured all of family life for us. Our whole family system was marked by it. Is it any wonder that all of us kids, now adults, struggled and struggle still with intimacy and affection and attachment issues? Is it any wonder that between the five of us there are so many failed and broken marriages and two that are same-sex marriages?

As a puzzled kid who grew up with a lot of whys, it all got real befuddling. But your answers don't emerge until years later because it takes that long to even figure out what the questions are. And by then, the damage is already done and evident in a thousand nuanced ways.

So Jacob was married to Rachel as well as Leah, and they had two boys, Joseph and Benjamin. And just as he favored one wife over the other, Jacob made no attempt to conceal the fact that he favored his two sons from Rachel, especially Joseph, more than any of his other kids. Benjamin was not in the picture on the goat-skinned tent wall because Rachel died giving birth to him. But Joseph, standing to Jacob's immediate right, was about fourteen at the time the picture was taken.

> Your answers don't emerge until years later because it takes that long to even figure out what the questions are.

Also in the picture was a woman named Bilhah; she was the handmaid, the servant girl of Rachel. During a time when Rachel and Leah were competing for who could have the most kids, Rachel gave her handmaid, Bilhah, to Jacob to tilt the baby-making odds in her favor.

And Jacob, like a bullied sheep, did what his jealous and manipulative wife wanted him to do. And Bilhah ended up having two boys for him, Dan and Naphtali.

Not to be outdone, Leah gave Jacob her handmaid, Zilpah, and she had two sons with Jacob, Gad and Asher. Jacob, weak and compliant, trapped by his own poor choices, just did what he was told, and family life got even more complex.

All in all, Jacob was married to Leah, a woman who all her life was made to feel second-class because her husband never really loved her. He was also married to Rachel, whom he really loved. And he was sort of married to the two hand-maids, each from a different race of people with altogether different, idolatrous religions. He had four boys with them (who were some kind of relation to the six boys), a girl with Leah, and two boys with Rachel.

What kind of family system can you construct out of polygamy, bitter jealousy, rivalry, favoritism, manipulation, unloved wives, and uncherished kids—all compounded by racial, ethnic, and religious diversity? I'll tell you what kind: one that plots to kill one of their brothers and ends up selling him as a slave.

Genesis 37 is the poisoned fruit of the preceding twelve chapters, which cover the earlier life of Jacob that I have just reviewed. This distorted and twisted maze of relation-ships is almost laughable were it not so painful. Imagine the tension and spite and bitterness that charged this household with an electricity of dysfunction.

And now imagine this household led by a man who no longer had any moral authority in his own home: who was clearly manipulated by his wives and openly discounted, disregarded, and discredited by his sons. In this sense, Jacob walked with a limp long before he ever wrestled with the angel of the Lord (see Genesis 32). For all the number of kids he fathered, Jacob was actually a parental eunuch, rendered impotent as a father by his own flawed choices. I guess being chosen and called by God face-to-face doesn't guarantee a sparkling future. Where there is a human will involved, there is always a way to make a mess of things.

What can we learn from this kind of mess? Well, for husbands, we learn that the best, most securing thing you can give your children is to love their mother exclusively. And wives, the best, most encouraging thing you can give your children is respect for their father.

The lack of exclusive marital love and deep marital respect in Joseph's family led to the polygamy that divided it. Polygamy is uncommon in our day. But divorce is not. You might even say that in our time, divorce has become a kind of serialized polygamy. And the pain of Jacob's household has long been the pain of our nation's household. Our whole national fabric is ripped and torn by it. And to our sorrow, the church has become no exception to the rule.

Think of the pain that creased the clan of Jacob because of his polygamy. And now think of the pain of families torn apart by divorce. Some of us don't have to think of the pain: we've lived it. Or are still living it. And a lot of us didn't choose it. The choice was imposed on us. As Thomas Lynch wrote in *The Undertaking* when his wife divorced him and moved away, "I was 'awarded' custody—four badly saddened kids I felt a failure toward."[2]

> You might even say that in our time, divorce has become a kind of serialized polygamy.

Few of us in this world go untouched by divorce or family breakdown. There are likely only one or two degrees of separation between us and a broken marriage in our wider families. My own kids have triplet cousins they have never seen. And they'll likely never be anything more than a family statistic because, multiple relationship fractures later, they are far beyond the reach of Facebook or any other means of even finding them.

And all of us are the poorer for it. Why? Because, in some way, the blood in my veins and in the veins of my kids runs in theirs. That must count for more than a tired shrug of resignation. Take any picture in any family album and start erasing people's faces and soon their lives follow and our memory of them fades and something in our own lives just empties out. Put a name on it . . . I can't. Maybe the word is *poverty*—a poverty of closeness and affection and meaningful, family love.

Let me say these few things, if I can. When the Bible says God hates divorce, God doesn't hate divorce because He is holy any more than a husband hates cancer because he is healthy. A husband hates cancer because he sees what the cruel pain of cancer does to his wife. And God hates divorce because He sees what the cruel pain of divorce does to His children.

You who read my words in this moment who are divorced, know this: God sees your tears and He sorrows with you. Psalm 56:8 says that God keeps our tears in a bottle (NASB); and for some of us, that bottle is pretty full by now. But God is on your side in rebuilding life. The pain you endure in these days is not God punishing you. It is the inevitable pain that comes with divorce.

And in the midst of it, God is for you. He knows you worry yourself sick over your kids. But remember: *out of the mess that was Jacob's household, God brought Joseph—one of the most winsome and beautiful lives in all the Bible.*

Don't think that because your family is creased or wounded by divorce, God can't still bring a Joseph out of your household. God is never limited by our failing choices or the choices that others have recklessly imposed on us. There are second-choice lives we are compelled to live, lives we would never have chosen but that have been imposed upon us in a fallen world. But, always remember that there are no second-class lives in the kingdom of God.

> God doesn't hate divorce because He is holy . . . God hates divorce because He sees what the cruel pain of divorce does to His children.

I have learned over the years in pastoral life that God has the back of every brokenhearted parent struggling through the mess of fractured family life. I have watched Him do what Isaiah gave witness to in Isaiah 61:3: bring beauty from ashes, bring the oil of gladness out of a season of mourning, and give a garment of praise for the spirit of heaviness. He will walk you into a new day. For He who said His eye in on the sparrow also said you are worth more than many sparrows.

Years ago, as a teenage boy, I spent a rainy Saturday afternoon watching a National Geographic special on a grainy black-and-white TV. It was about tribal life in some southern region of Africa. While I cannot remember the name of the particular country or tribe, the name of the chief of the tribe I remember well: the great chief Anga Gaga Tongola III.

In a scene that sticks with me still, the great chief, who was now potbellied and old, sat in front of his grass hut surrounded by a number of wives and children of all ages, sizes, and shapes. Meanwhile, standing off to the side, were a number of younger men, all looking like young lions, seemingly pacing and waiting to strike. The astute interviewer asked through the interpreter if the old chief was worried about the presence of these younger men. Did he fear they might want to get rid of him and take over the rule of the tribe?

I have never forgotten his answer. "The task of the chief" he said, "is not to survive, but to ensure the survival of his people." That Jacob's tribe survives is a tribute to the absolute grace and mercy of God. But because of Jacob's many flawed choices, it's a survival marked with many tears, much pain, and deep brokenness. Could it be that our family tribe needn't suffer as his did? Is there a better way to *do* family? God seems to think so.

When Dreams Become Nightmares

✦ Genesis 37:12-20 ✦

"Which of you fathers, if your son asks for a fish, will give him a snake instead?"

—LUKE 11:11

"It is our choices, Harry, that show what we truly are, far more than our abilities."[1]

—ALBUS DUMBLEDORE,
HARRY POTTER AND THE CHAMBER OF SECRETS

WHAT WAS YOUR dream growing up? Did you become the actress or writer or singer or athlete you dreamed you would? Maybe you dreamed you'd be a wealthy business-person or an Air Force pilot. Children's dreams are full of wonder and promise and hope. One of the great features of American life and culture is the American dream: that anyone can grow up and find a better life, a bigger life, perhaps even become the president. (No, given our day, that would be nightmare!)

Back before Al Gore was inventing the Internet, I was growing up in the frozen north known as Canada. Canadians take a lot of grief about how cold it is up there, because frankly, a lot of the time it is cold. Like last year. We had a great summer. It came on a Tuesday. We tease ourselves about it a lot, saying things like, "We have four seasons in Canada: hockey season, ski season, snowmobile season, and ice fishing season." So while American children dream of moving up, we dream of moving south. Anywhere warm will do. Now that I actually live in the South, I can fully affirm that God had a place in my childhood dreams.

But did God have a place in Joseph's dreams? When you know the end of the story, it tends to drain the drama from it like a lukewarm bath. Since we know how the Joseph story ends, it's hard for us to imagine what his family thought about the source of his dreams when he spoke of them. Did God really give Joseph the dreams he had, or did Joseph just imagine his own future as he preferred it to be? Like a boy who dreams of being a major-league pitcher and falls asleep dreaming of pitching in the World Series, did Joseph construct his own dreams? Or were his dreams a projection of what his father preferred the future to be? The text holds the answers to these questions.

In his book *The Sibling Effect*, Jeffrey Kluger wrote, "One of the worst-kept secrets of family life [is] that every parent has a preferred son or daughter."[2] He also counsels parents to just keep quiet about it. Too bad Jacob never got to read the book. With only so much parental love and attention to go around, children naturally compete for their share. Jacob just outright and openly gave the full measure of his love and affection to Joseph.

> "One of the worst-kept secrets of family life [is] that every parent has a preferred son or daughter."
> —Jeffrey Kluger

Almost every child assumes the old Tommy Smothers line is true: "Mom always liked you best." In other words, kids are certain *some* sibling was loved more than they. In Joseph's case, it went undisguised. Jacob openly favored Joseph over his brothers. Favoritism is always divisive and toxic in family life. The text does not mince words: they hated Joseph for it (Genesis 37:4). And the distance between that hatred and what they thought of their father was not far. It would be a stake in the ground that they would never forget.

How crippling is it? Later in his book, Kluger tells the story of Charles Dickens, whose sister was sent to school while he was sent to work in a boot-blacking factory. He was scarred by the experience of being the least-favored sibling. Years later, as a celebrated and adored adult, Dickens would write, "My whole nature was so penetrated by the grief and humiliation of [it] that even now, famous and caressed and happy, I . . . wander desolate back to that time in my life."[3]

There has never been a kid who didn't think that he or she was the neglected one or that dad or mom always liked one of his or her siblings more. The Smothers Brothers got that one right. There is not much you can do about that.

But part of what it means to not to provoke your kids to anger (Ephesians 6:4 NASB), so far as it depends on you, is to treat each of your children with an equality of love, affection, and interest. It's a very hard scale to balance, but it must be worked at. Because some of our kids are just easier to love and it takes less work to love them, we can find ourselves defaulting toward them. Let Jacob be a cautionary tale for you and me because parental favoritism is toxic to any family system.

Even as bad a husband as he was at times, Jacob didn't need to lose his sons. But he lost any chance for their respect by shamelessly favoring Joseph over them.

Now, it must be said that Jacob comes by his penchant for favoritism honestly; he learned it from his own mother. Genesis 27 shows us how his mother, Rebekah, favored him over his brother, Esau, and conspired with him to deceive their father, Isaac, so Jacob could steal Esau's birthright. Jacob lost two decades of closeness with his father's family over that. He never did get those old relationships back. Rachel was the favored wife for years, and now, in Genesis 37, Jacob will lose his son with her for decades by repeating the same parental mistake of his mother.

In the eyes of Jacob, the sons of Leah (Bilhah and Zilpah, Joseph's half brothers) were the redheaded stepchildren when compared to the favored Joseph. As parents, we are meant to build platforms of relationship with each of our children from which to launch them into their future. Jacob built the kind of parenting platforms from which his ten unfavored sons, born of Leah, were just pushed off. While Jacob was setting Joseph up for life, he was setting the rest of his boys up to fail. Genesis 37 would read completely different if Jacob hadn't emotionally handicapped the whole family with his favoritism of Joseph.

To add fuel to the fire of hate, Joseph ratted out his half brothers and brought home a bad report about them. Then, even before the dreams became an issue, there was the whole matter of the ornamental robe: the unique gift from Jacob that was the tangible, visible emblem of his father's favoritism. Joseph wore it everywhere to the effect that his brothers felt he was constantly rubbing their noses in the paternal favor he enjoyed.

> While Jacob was setting Joseph up for life, he was setting the rest of his boys up to fail.

To them, it was as if they wore Walmart jeans and Kmart sandals while Joseph walked around in designer jeans and carried a Gucci man bag over his shoulder to hold his cell phone and iPad. But actually, it was even more than that.

In the early nineteenth century, Joseph H. Hertz was the chief rabbi of the United Kingdom. He commented on this text that the ornamental robe given to Joseph was a chieftain's robe, the kind worn by Semitic clan rulers of that time period. The robe itself was an insignia of rulership. It was not just an elegant gift to a favored son. In giving it to Joseph, Jacob was marking out Joseph as his heir apparent to lead the tribal clan, even before he was dead. He openly chose Joseph over his brothers, passing over the cultural custom that would have given that ruling role to Reuben, who was the eldest.

In doing this, Jacob was trying to put his authoritative stamp on a future he would never inhabit but which he felt he could not entrust to any of his other sons. History would vindicate his choice. As the story unfolds, none of the other sons prove themselves worthy. As my preaching mentor, Dr. Ellsworth Kalas, once remarked, Jacob probably thought the other ten sons came from Esau's side of the gene pool. They were men of impulse and passion, men of appetites, not sound moral judgment. In making the choice early, it was as if Jacob sensed he couldn't wait. There was some sense in him that realized he was losing ground in moral and paternal authority over his sons. He was slipping, so he leveraged what power he had left to position Joseph to lead the family after he was gone.

Imagine the tension among the brothers that this created. It would be similar to having your father announce at the supper table one night that one of the children (and it's not you!) is being given the family home when mom and dad die, and the rest of you will only get whatever scraps fall off the table of the will. Each one of Jacob's sons felt judged, weighed in the balances, and found wanting. They felt devalued, overlooked, and passed over. I think you'd be familiar with that feeling. Anyone would. Then the tension was taken deeper by Joseph's dreams.

Jacob and Joseph shared a number of things in common. Both were dreamers; both were household favorites; both cut in front of cultural custom and took over the leadership of the family tribe. They were similar in this as well: they had the relational savvy and the sensitivity of an eggplant when it came to the life circumstance in which they found themselves. On one hand, Joseph couldn't stop himself from talking about his grandiose dreams of superiority over his brothers. Don't you want to just reach between the lines of your Bible and tell Joseph to put a lid on it? On the other hand, beginning with the dreams, we discover Jacob couldn't stop putting Joseph's life in danger.

When Jacob gave Joseph the cloak of a chieftain, that "coat of many colors," everyone understood he was, in effect, being anointed as the next leader of the family tribe. Jacob's act didn't just alienate Joseph from his brothers; it stimulated something in Joseph's heart. It created a vision for his life that he would never have considered, given the customs tied to birth order. The dreams followed because they were generated and influenced by Jacob's choice.

The dreams that came to Joseph did have a divine, predictive element to them. They would come to pass. But Joseph's dreams also had a human element that could not be set aside. They were really the dreams of his father and the preferred future Jacob wanted for the family. Jacob put a future on Joseph that shaped his dreams, but it also deeply crippled his everyday life. With that choice Joseph was positioned in family life as a lightning rod for his brothers' hatred.

If you pause here and look at the story from a slightly different angle, you can see how it is a cautionary tale for any parent. We can limit, frustrate, or perhaps even imperil our children's development by imposing our dreams upon them. We've all seen how disfiguring it can be. You find parents trying to live vicariously through their children, keeping the dreams of their own childhood alive—only it's killing their child's own dreams. At other times, you'll find parents forcing their child down a path the child has no passion for, interest in, or calling for in life. The better part of parental wisdom is to fuel your children's own dreams, not give them yours.

Jacob, who was clearly aware of his family's dynamics, nevertheless put Joseph's life in greater danger a second time when he sent Joseph out to check on the brothers who despised him. The last time Joseph checked on them in verse 2, he brought back a bad report on them; he essentially snitched on them. I'm sure they would have loved a visit from the homegrown tattletale.

To make it even worse, Jacob sent Joseph wearing the ornamental robe. I want to grab Jacob by the collar and say, "Jacob, what were you thinking?" but I already know he was obviously not thinking. Why not just pin a sign on Joseph: "Here's the brother you hate! I'm far away back at home! Do what you like with him!" It's like asking your teenage daughter who hates her little sister to babysit her while you go on a cruise with your wife. How many Hollywood movies are variations on that theme? It's a disaster in the making.

But then, if you can imagine, it got even worse. In Genesis 34, Jacob's one daughter, Dinah, was defiled in Shechem; she was virtually raped. The lord of that city thought he'd make a deal to cover it up. The man who did it would take Dinah as his wife, and the two people groups would settle in together and share the land, intermarry, and live happily ever after as a bigger people group.

The text says in Genesis 34:13 that Jacob's sons replied deceitfully (I wonder where they learned that!). They spoke with the lord of Shechem and said all the men of the city would have to be circumcised before they could enter into such an intertribal agreement.

Three days after the ordeal of circumcision, while the men of Shechem were incapacitated, the sons of Jacob (led by Simeon and Levi) went into town and killed all the young men, taking all the women and children, the livestock, and all their possessions. Jacob said to his boys in 34:30, "You have brought trouble upon me by making me odious to the inhabitants of the land" (NRSV). I should think so.

Now, back to chapter 37, and where does Jacob send Joseph to go look for his brothers? Shechem! Picking up on Jesus' words from Luke 11, Joseph was in need of a fish and Jacob was handing him a snake. Joseph couldn't help but be bitten by the circumstance that was unfolding.

The problem only deepened when Joseph got lost. Can you imagine him asking for directions in good Hebrew? Joseph said to the nearest man he could find (and there aren't that many!), "Hi. I'm Jacob's boy. Have you seen my brothers who slaughtered all the young men in your town? They're grazing some sheep . . . a lot of which they stole from you."

Jacob sent Joseph into the animosity of his brothers and the animosity of these offended people. Not to be outdone, he dressed him for the occasion so he couldn't be missed. Here I think Jacob's name should mean "Big Idiot!" Why not just cover Joseph with honey and throw him into a den of grizzly bears?

Jacob's terrible judgment to send Joseph out to check on his brothers loosened a stone that started a landslide in the family. The effect of that decision would be a cascade of pain and regret that would last for decades and decades in Jacob's soul. He ended up emotionally paralyzed and crippled almost until the day he died.

The floor of my house has a creak or two in it. I don't notice it much until it's late at night and I'm letting the cat out and I don't want to awaken "the queen" who is snoozing away beside me. When I hear the floor squeak, I say to myself, "I have got to get under the house and fix that. I've got to shim those spots up a bit."

> Jacob's terrible judgment loosened a stone that started a landslide in the family.

Learn this well: sound judgment in leading a family comes when a parent listens to his or her household. What is your household saying to you in the night? When you lie there in the dark and think back over your day and consider your tomorrows, what is your household saying to you? As parents, we must pay attention to the creaks and squeaks and sounds of our family's life.

There are times when we need to stop and ask ourselves, Is this working? Is our family working? Where are the stress points? What am I missing? What needs to change? As parents, we must be intentional about assessing the state of family life in order to demonstrate our care and concern for each of the children.

That takes time, of course. The old myth is that if we have quality time with our kids, then that's enough to stay engaged in their lives. But quality time is not something you can schedule like a lunch appointment. Truth be told, *quality time emerges in the midst of quantity time.* Be around. Be fully present to them in the moments you are with them. It's the only way to pick up on clues and hints . . . to catch the mood or take the family pulse.

Now, for every single parent reading this, I can only imagine the pressure this brings. Life is unusually draining for the single parent. Could it be that part of what it means to help single folks parent well is for the church to promote many-handed parenting? Could it be that the rest of us need to be alert to that and help out single parents where we can?

A further significant way to stay engaged in your children's lives is to not just get into their lives, but invite them into yours. Bring them into the family decision-making process whenever you can. You might find out that they really don't enjoy going to your brother-in-law's for Thanksgiving or riding in the back of a minivan. Kids will surprise you with their insights. In hearing them, in listening to them, you will find they take fuller ownership of family life and will want to find other ways to contribute.

> Don't just get into your children's lives; invite them into yours.

It can be discouraging trying to find an entry point to begin to make changes. You may well feel that you cannot do what others can. Remember: no one gets it all right. And, know this: every family is dysfunctional. It's only a matter of degree. My wife, Marilyn, came from a dysfunctional Christian home, and I came from a dysfunctional home where belief was never practiced. Our family systems offered almost nothing we wanted to pattern our family life after.

By intention, we said that we would start a new tribe, and we did. We made mistakes, to be certain, but we like to think that at least they were original mistakes! We got help where we could. We got advice from other parents, especially from those just a little further down the road than us. We made a plan, established a handful of principles we'd operate family life by, and got as strategic in our parenting as we did with our money or career planning.

Parenting is not intuitive, like eating or sleeping. It takes intentionality and some real sweat. In our household we say that marriage is a commitment to doing the work of life together. Family life takes an equal commitment to simply work at it till you work it out. You don't want to default to the old patterns that were a stake that held you back for years.

All of our children are married now, and all of them have built their own tribes. We told them early in the game that our goal for them was that they would do that. They did learn a few things from our good choices and profited by watching us cope with the mistakes we made. We are blessed when we see how they have built some new ways of dealing with tribal life that we would never have thought of. And as the parents, I can tell you how we are quietly honored when we see parts of their tribes' lives that reflect the tribe we built.

I think giving our kids such freedom is wonderfully empowering for them. It's still early; the last chapters haven't been written in their tribal stories. But so far, none of them has sent their Joseph out to get abused by his brothers.

Speaking of Joseph, he's not the brightest bulb in the socket, is he? Or as my daughter Rachel would say, "He's not the sharpest duck in the herd."

He's about seventeen in Genesis 37, and you'd think he might have been smart enough not to be a tattletale. What kid doesn't know that even if the parents get involved and intervene to shield him from payback, later on the siblings are going to get even?

His dimness list is pretty long: wearing that coat everywhere; wearing it to go to Shechem; telling his brothers not once but twice about his grandiose dreams. Joseph was a walking can of gas, going around pouring himself on fires that were already burning out of control. It's a miracle that he made it through to Genesis 38.

I tried to chalk all this up to him being naive. But my head wouldn't fully go there. Then I tried to chalk it up to the fact that he never got to listen to the James Dobson adolescence tapes with his dad, but that too was a big stretch.

Then I figured it out. He was seventeen. He was behaving like a seventeen-year-old. I remember being that age. I was just as dimly naive and unaware as he was. Why? Because I was seventeen; that's why!

In Genesis 37, Joseph had a bad case of being seventeen. If he were alive today, living where I do in Kentucky, and he did what he did, you know what people would say? "You know that Joseph? He snitched on his brothers and they beat the tar outta him, bless his heart."

> Marriage is a commitment to doing the work of life together.

Or they might say something like, "You know that Joseph? He went off to New York City on his own last week and got on the subway at midnight with twenty-dollar bills pinned to his jacket, and you know what? He got robbed, bless his heart."

Now, you know what "bless his heart" means, don't you? It's a Southernism that means, "What an idiot!" As in, "Jimmy was trying to impress his girl and drove his daddy's car into a pole at the end of the street, bless his heart!" Of course Jimmy did that. Jimmy is seventeen.

I've learned over time to expect age-appropriate maturity and behavior from kids. I try not to get to wound up if kids don't act like little adults. So I don't expect my four-year-old grandson to show much restraint with a water gun in his hand. I don't expect my preadolescent granddaughters to completely understand why they can't have boys come to the campout in our backyard. Seventeen-year-olds can only have seventeen years' worth of maturity and sensitivity. To expect more of them is to expect too much.

And do remember to factor this into the equation about Joseph: his mother, Rachel, died when he was fifteen. His grief and his emotional wounds from that were still pretty raw. And the other women of the household had no interest in him; he was the son of their rival. They were of no maternal comfort to him. His father was not given to nurturing, and his other behaviors betrayed how he was just not sensitive to Joseph's needs. And we all know how his brothers felt. Joseph was very much alone on an island of his grief and loss.

> I've learned over time to expect age-appropriate maturity and behavior from kids.

Then, when he was sixteen, only a year later, his beloved grandfather, Isaac, died. His world was being shook. How might you expect a boy to handle all of that? I know folks in their thirties, forties, and fifties who still haven't processed the death of a parent or grandparent. He was just a boy with adult-sized losses to figure out.

You and I? We have our own losses. As it did for Joseph, *sometimes it will take years for us to fully discover that for every loss there's an Easter with our name on it.* So on one hand, you have to let Joseph be seventeen. But on the other hand, there is no reason for you or me to be Jacob and make choices that make family life worse than it already is. 'Cause after all, you and I are the normal ones in our family, remember? Bless our hearts!

The Soap-Opera Life
✦ Genesis 37:17b–36 ✦

"So he got up and went to his father.
"But while he was still a long way off, his father saw him
and was filled with compassion for him; he ran to his
son, threw his arms around him and kissed him."

—LUKE 15:20

We have to distrust each other. It's our only defense
against betrayal.

—TENNESSEE WILLIAMS

IN AN ODD conversation with a grocery store clerk this past
week, the topic of soap operas came up. I was standing in the
checkout line and came face-to-face with what appeared to
me to be about a dozen soap-opera magazines. I remember
from my mother's days when she would hurry home from the
store to watch her "stories." But I am so disconnected from
that world today, I wondered aloud to the clerk if daytime
soaps were still on TV.

"Oh yeah" she replied, popping her gum. "I take my
lunch at two o'clock so I can watch 'em in the staff room."

Not wanting to comment on her artistic taste in television programming, I let the conversation go. But I thought to myself, *How can anyone watch that stuff?* I mean, isn't life as it is portrayed on soap operas *so life giving, so very life affirming, and so very meaningfully genuine?* Sure . . . and Bill Gates is buying stock in Apple.

Curiously, when you read the life of Joseph, you discover it has a soap-opera kind of feel. A Joseph soap opera would be prime-time stuff: deception and intrigue, betrayals and lies, and, of course, infidelity of the worst kind. And that is just what happens in the last twenty verses of Genesis 37.

So Joseph went after his brothers and found them near Dothan. But they saw him in the distance, and before he reached them, they plotted to kill him.

"Here comes that dreamer!" they said to each other. "Come now, let's kill him and throw him into one of these cisterns and say that a ferocious animal devoured him. Then we'll see what comes of his dreams."

When Reuben heard this, he tried to rescue him from their hands. "Let's not take his life," he said. "Don't shed any blood. Throw him into this cistern here in the wilderness, but don't lay a hand on him." Reuben said this to rescue him from them and take him back to his father.

So when Joseph came to his brothers, they stripped him of his robe—the ornate robe he was wearing—and they took him and threw him into the cistern. The cistern was empty; there was no water in it.

As they sat down to eat their meal, they looked up and saw a caravan of Ishmaelites coming from Gilead. Their camels were loaded with spices, balm and myrrh, and they were on their way to take them down to Egypt.

Judah said to his brothers, "What will we gain if we kill our brother and cover up his blood? Come, let's sell him to the Ishmaelites and not lay our hands on him; after all, he is our brother, our own flesh and blood." His brothers agreed.

So when the Midianite merchants came by, his brothers pulled Joseph up out of the cistern and sold him for twenty shekels of silver to the Ishmaelites, who took him to Egypt.

When Reuben returned to the cistern and saw that Joseph was not there, he tore his clothes. He went back to his brothers and said, "The boy isn't there! Where can I turn now?"

Then they got Joseph's robe, slaughtered a goat and dipped the robe in the blood. They took the ornate robe back to their father and said, "We found this. Examine it to see whether it is your son's robe."

He recognized it and said, "It is my son's robe! Some ferocious animal has devoured him. Joseph has surely been torn to pieces."

Then Jacob tore his clothes, put on sackcloth and mourned for his son many days. All his sons and daughters came to comfort him, but he refused to be comforted. "No," he said, "I will continue to mourn until I join my son in the grave." So his father wept for him.

Meanwhile, the Midianites sold Joseph in Egypt to Potiphar, one of Pharaoh's officials, the captain of the guard. (Gen. 37:17b–36)

Here's your typical soap opera scene: there's this handsome guy with a name like Brock. He unexpectedly bumps into his girlfriend, Jessica, at a party. Jessica knows that Brock has been cheating on her with Karen. But Brock knows that Jessica has been cheating on him with Lance.

So they both stare at each other with feigned surprise as the camera moves in, 'cause we all know that they both know, and we're just waiting so see who is going to say what about who, what, and where, and when, and why. And the tension is building and their lips are quivering and their eyes are riveted on each other, the music builds and builds, and . . . and . . . then we break for a commercial!

Man, if I weren't a pastor, I could write this stuff! But the writer of Genesis does a better job than I ever could. Because in this badly messed-up, dysfunctional family of Jacob, there is more betrayal and intrigue in the story of the sale of Joseph into slavery than we can ever imagine. And like the soaps, it all began to take shape a couple of episodes . . . uh, excuse me . . . chapters ago.

It all began with Reuben. He was the firstborn of Jacob, the one who by culture and custom was the entitled one. He was the one with all the status that came from being the first-born, the one who got the lion's share of the father's blessing and estate. Reuben was the one with all the clout in family life. He was meant to be, as it were, lord over his brothers.

> Reuben ought to have been the pride and joy of his father. But he was not. He was Reuben, the unwanted son of the unloved Leah.

American novelist Don Snyder wrote in his autobiographical work, *Of Time and Memory*, "Let us hope that we are all preceded in this world by a love story."[1] Reuben was not. His grandfather Laban deceived Jacob by slipping his daughter Leah into the marriage bed of Jacob after a wedding night of feasting and drinking, though Jacob had worked seven years for Rachel. But "[Jacob] loved Rachel more than Leah" (Gen. 29:30 NASB), and Reuben paid the price for that all his life.

As the firstborn son to Jacob and Leah, Reuben ought to have been the pride and joy of his father. But he was not.

Why? Because he was born to Jacob's unloved and uncherished wife, Leah. He was not Reuben, the darling firstborn son. He was Reuben, the unwanted son of the unloved Leah.

If you are Reuben, and you are living every day with a reference point for your value being your younger but favored brother Joseph, you can see how he would easily come to despise both Joseph and Jacob his father.

In the classic movie *The Godfather Part II*, there is a scene where the younger brother, Michael, who is now the don of the Corleone family, is making a move to diminish his older brother, Fredo's, place in the family. And in words you can hear coming right off the lips of Reuben, Fredo shouts at Michael, through bitter tears, saying he was passed over even though he was the older brother, and now he wants the respect that should go with being the older brother. But instead of respect, he got a death sentence.

Reuben grew up being made to feel second best, the stepped-over one. He was the second-best, uncherished son born of a second-best, uncherished wife. Reuben could do nothing to supplant Joseph in his father's eyes. So he did what a lot of sons have done: he tried to supplant Jacob himself.

Every father who has a son knows he has an alpha male problem on his hands. It's when his boys start to win when they wrestle with the old man. Naturalists have carefully documented the idea of the alpha male as seen among gorillas. The old silverback is continually challenged by the young males for primacy of the gorilla band.

And I remember well when that happened for me with my seventeen-year-old son, Ben. We were sparring good-naturedly on the front deck of our house when he got a little more serious about the tussle and was clearly exerting all he had to defeat me. And he was also clearly winning, ready to claim alpha male status as a rite of passage, if nothing else.

Then, just when it appeared he might win, I did what most fathers would do. I reached down and took hold of him where a father should never take hold of his grown son. He was both shocked and paralyzed by the move. While he was hollering about how I was cheating, I hurled him over the railing. When the laughter died down and we were pouring lemonade together, I responded to his feigned protest with sage wisdom: "Old and crafty beats younger and stronger any day."

Let me tell you what an alpha male challenge might look like in Old Testament times. Do you remember the account of Absalom usurping the throne from his father, David, in 2 Samuel 16? To demonstrate that he had completely taken over his father's role as leader, one of the first things Absalom did was pitch a tent on the roof of his house and publicly sleep with each of David's wives and concubines. He was staking out his turf. It was Absalom's way of demonstrating that he was the alpha male in charge now.

In Genesis 35, Reuben tried the same thing. I believe he was trying to unseat his father as the leader of the tribe. In verse 22 we read, "While Israel [Jacob] was living in [the region of Migdal Eder], Reuben went in and slept with his father's concubine Bilhah, and Israel [Jacob] heard of it."

> Jacob was paralyzed by his past, and he did nothing, hoping it would all just drift away on the wind.

He heard of it, but Jacob did nothing about it. I believe that Reuben was trying to wrestle control of the family clan away from his father in a fashion intended to humiliate his father and expose him for his weakness. Yet Jacob did nothing. He did nothing to punish his son or chastise him. Why?

Well, if he did act on his son's indiscretion, he would have to openly face the challenge of Reuben in the eyes of his family. He was already an old man. He was already discounted in the eyes of the family for his weakness as a father. What if the family sided with the new alpha male? What if all the brothers who knew the rest of Jacob's weaknesses, all his flaws and failures, so well, favored Reuben over him?

Add to this his favoritism for Joseph. In doing this, Jacob had already lost his moral authority in his own home. Can we be honest here? If you subtracted Jacob's skills as a shrewd livestock entrepreneur from who he was, there wouldn't be much left to admire. He had no moral weight. In that sense, he felt all the more powerless to act and punish Reuben. Like all poor fathers, Jacob was paralyzed by his past, and he did nothing, hoping it would all just drift away on the wind. But, of course, it didn't.

Criticism is a cheap gift but a common one in pastoral life. Pastoral work is so very public, and it makes you an easy target. At such times I take comfort in

> The Bible was right again: the truth did set me free.

the old saying about criticism. "Sometimes it's like being a [Texas mule] in a hail storm. You just have to hunker down and take it."

But betrayal is another matter altogether. Something has to be done about betrayals when they happen. I remember a time when a man started a rumor that I was sleeping with a prominent woman in the church. There is enough malice in that sort of betrayal to cripple a church for a generation.

I took an elder and went to his door. And no, he didn't invite me in. There on his front porch I told him face-to-face that I knew he had started the rumor and that it was sin to do so. But I also told him I knew the Bible taught that I was to forgive him. I set my will, formed the words, and told him I forgave him. I then said it was up to him to respond as God would have him respond. And his response was to close the door and never come back to church again.

The psalmist David caught the sense of it all so well when he wrote of Ahithophel's betrayal of him in Psalm 55:12–14: "If an enemy were insulting me, I could endure it; if a foe were rising against me, I could hide. But it is you, a man like myself, my companion, my close friend, with whom I once enjoyed sweet fellowship at the house of God, as we walked about among the worshipers."

Many years later, I was speaking at an event, and that man stopped me in the corridor to say hello. It was my Ahithophel. And you know what? I was surprised to find how much I genuinely loved seeing him. In simply forgiving him years ago, I was released by God from any sense of bitterness or grudge-bearing. The Bible was right again: the truth did set me free. Confronting that betrayal in a biblical manner completely changed the future of that relationship.

Betrayals like Reuben's just don't drift off on the wind. They have to be confronted—in love and on biblical terms. When they are not, you get relational climate change. You end up with a chill coming over the marriage bed, a cold frost settling over the workplace, a north wind that freezes hearts blowing through family life. We all know such experiences and such days. How's the weather in your world?

Still, for countless reasons, some of which we'll never know, Jacob didn't confront the betrayal. Imagine it, then: every time Reuben and his father came face-to-face, they both knew that the other one knew. It's Brock and Jessica all over again, only it's not a TV soap. It's real life.

Reality television has given us humiliation as art. Sitcoms are fueled by it and commonly run on shame-based humor. If what happened on a sitcom happened in your world, you'd be mopping up the blood for years. But on television, they just break to a commercial. It never really gets resolved. Real life doesn't work that way, does it? Real life needs resolution or real life is just an ongoing, open wound.

Well, Jacob never pressed for that resolution. Life went on, of course, because that's what life does. Only it was never the same again. How could it be? From that day forward, Reuben and Jacob looked at each other in that struggling, awkward way. The silences that passed between them left unspoken thoughts hanging hamstrung in the air.

And you have to imagine that the whole family found out what happened. What did Wendell Berry write in *Jayber Crow* about small-town life in the South? "Around here it's hard for an interesting secret to stay secret."[2] It becomes the secret everyone knows but no one can talk about. Life is a soap-opera scene every day. It becomes the elephant in the tent of which no one speaks.

But it's there. It's there in the looks that get passed around the campfire at night. It's lurking on the edge of a remark made by a brother who knows. It floats across a face that smirks at the mention of a name.

In *The Canterbury Tales*, Geoffrey Chaucer wrote, "A guilty man thinks everybody only talks of him."[3] Every time Reuben walked into the presence of his brothers, he was tied up in guilty knots, wondering if they were talking about him or about what he did. Not that this ever happens to you or me. Ouch.

Chaucer was right, of course: unprocessed guilt is all-consuming, especially for Reuben. He had defiled his father's bed; everyone knew he was guilty, and the guilt just hung in the air like toxic fumes, poisoning the atmosphere of the whole family.

As in the earlier illustration from my own family of origin, where my parents secret of a 'shot gun' wedding crippled our family with a legacy of shame, we learn that secrets have power. It is always a deformative power. They misshape us. The power of a secret, even a badly kept one, is the formational force of the scene in Genesis 37. This badly kept secret of Reuben defiling his father's bed was behind all of his behavior in this chapter.

> The power of a secret—its ability to control us—dies in light of transparent honesty and forgiveness.

If he had dealt with his sin in a genuine way, repented and sought forgiveness from his father, and been restored to his father, the secret would have been powerless to control him.

The power of a secret—its ability to control us—dies in the light of transparent honesty and forgiveness. But Reuben's secret remained in the dark, and he was, in effect, caught and trapped in the darkness with it.

To no one's surprise, Reuben's alpha male plan didn't work. The ingenuity of an illegitimate response to life's hurts and wounds never produces the results it imagines. If you do the work of genuine repentance and forgiveness, it produces life-giving, life-affirming results. But Reuben's way of handling life produced only deeper pain and deformation of the family.

Not only did he not get what he wanted, he lost what he had. He lost what little favor he had left with his father. He lost face with his brothers. His very life was covered in humiliating shame. His brothers could sense it, and they probably played on it. I wonder what Dan and Naphtali thought of their brother sleeping with their mother. It became part of the already dysfunctional family ethos.

And Reuben lost his birthright. In Genesis 49:4, when Jacob was handing out blessings on his deathbed, he condemned Reuben for his act of shame and publicly took away his status as firstborn. His brothers saw this coming from a long way back. The guilt and shame of it were too unsparing to go unnoticed.

Guilt is private shame. Shame is guilt that goes public. And both are cruelly disfiguring. And both are at work here in this scene in Genesis 37 where Reuben appeared to be trying to help Joseph. When you read verses 21–22, you get every impression that Reuben was trying to save Joseph. It sounds so very noble of him until you realize he was only trying to recover the ground he had lost in the betrayal of his father.

When you see Reuben apparently mourning over the loss of Joseph in verses 29–30, it's a loss of a different kind that had him wailing. It was the loss of his opportunity to ingratiate himself back into his father's goodwill.

When you know the soap-opera story behind the story, what Reuben was doing had little to do with Joseph's welfare. It was not about Joseph. It was all about Reuben . . . as sin always is: it's all about "me."

To Reuben, Joseph was not a brother in need of rescue; he was a meal ticket back into his father's favor. Saving Joseph would get him back all he had lost. But in losing Joseph, he lost his best chance at restoration with Jacob.

Reuben's motive was transparently self-serving and fueled by *the private shame* of his own guilt. And *the public guilt* of sleeping with the mother of two of his brothers, which shamed him daily, was something he was trying to get rid of forever.

But his plan went south when his brothers sold Joseph to the Midianites, who were heading south. "Where can I turn now?" he cried in verse 30. Where indeed? He's just lost his way to his father's heart. Now he would never recover the ground he lost. And biblical history shows us that he never did.

Reuben found out that a non-genuine, soap-opera-values life just doesn't work. He found out it's as hard to absolve yourself of your own guilt as it is to sit in your own lap. Reuben found that guilt with his father couldn't be covered with good deeds or clever strategies.

Only genuine forgiveness can deal with the sins of non-genuine behavior. Such forgiveness enables us, as Buechner wrote, to "at long last finally finish with the past in the sense of removing its power over us to hurt us and other people and to stunt our growth as human beings."[4]

And you and I need to know that sins against our Father—our Father in heaven—cannot be covered with ingenuity or trying harder or clever ideas about paying Him back. Ever find yourself trying harder with God, doing more to please Him for all the wrong reasons, subconsciously trying to recover the ground you've lost and perhaps win a higher place in your Father's eyes?

It doesn't work that way. There are no substitutes for the menu of the divine order of things. Only genuine forgiveness can heal a relationship with your father and your Father in heaven. The non-genuine, soap-opera response cannot rid us of our guilt or restore a relationship. Only genuine repentance and forgiveness can give us back what we've lost to sin, which was the sweetness and the nearness of that relationship with Him.

Know this, now: God is still our Father, even when we sin, much as Jacob was still Reuben's father when Reuben sinned. The divine birth certificate hasn't changed. But there is a chill in the room because we have sinned against Him. There is this awkward coolness when we try to pray or try to worship. It's all just not working. We can't quite look Him in the eye anymore. Only genuine forgiveness can clean that mess up and restore the relationship.

In the Genesis narrative, as in any good writing, the story was being shaped toward the climax, when Joseph became the leader and savior of his family and his people. Up until then, it had been the firstborn who was the protector and preserver of the nation that was God's chosen people.

> God is still our Father, even when we sin, much as Jacob was still Reuben's father when Reuben sinned.

Isaac was the firstborn of Abraham. Jacob, who stole the birthright of Esau, thus became the de facto firstborn of Isaac. But then Reuben was disqualified entirely by his own sin, right? Well, not exactly. He was disqualified from his firstborn status by his own unwillingness to deal with his sin honestly and completely and transparently. And in all of these circumstances, in a sense, Jacob was already being set aside as leader, even before his death, by his own continued poor moral choices.

Who would step up to be the new alpha male since Reuben was disgraced? Simeon and Levi were second and third in the birth order after Reuben. But they disgraced the family by their leading role in the shameful destruction of Shechem.

Well, what about Judah? He was the fourth-born son. And at least he was trying to help Joseph in some measure in chapter 37. "Let's not kill him" he said. "Let's just sell him. After all, he *is* our brother." Good, virtuous, moral guy, right? Not so much.

The writer of Genesis will show us Judah's true character in the next chapter. Chapter 38 is an interlude in the narrative that seems to have no bearing on the development of Joseph's story. That is, until you read it as the writer's way of opening a window into Judah's heart and character.

In chapter 38, Judah, a widower at the time, slept with a temple prostitute of a pagan god, a prostitute who was actually his daughter-in-law in disguise . . . a daughter-in-law whom Judah had cheated by not providing a husband for her, as the law of the day required. Cheating, sex, incest, and deception all in one sentence. I told you this story is a soap opera!

Well, knowing *that* about his character in chapter 38 helps us interpret *what* he was doing there in chapter 37. In candor, he was in it for the money. While he appeared to be doing Joseph a selfless favor, he was really just trying to keep Joseph's blood off his hands and make some coin while doing it.

Although he appeared sincere, he was not, as proven by the next scene in chapter 37, when they all returned home to dad after the deed was done. Judah was in full agreement with the other brothers when they intentionally deceived their own father.

What's the old saying? Like father like son. These sons were like nuts that did not fall far from the paternal tree. They were a bunch of deceivers about to deceive the one whose name means "deceiver." It's a pattern of behavior we see often in this family.

Judah, along with the others, dipped Joseph's distinctive cloak in animal blood and presented it to Jacob as evidence of Joseph's death. Now, how could anyone be that callous? Well, in the same way calluses get built on our hands and feet, *sin builds calluses on our heart to the point where we lose any touch for tenderness* . . . we lose any and all sensitivity. Where do we see that here? We see it in the missing verse, the one that should come between verse 24 and verse 25. It's actually found in Genesis 42:21.

It was about twenty-two years later when these same brothers appeared before Joseph when he was the prime minister of Egypt. They bowed before him, just as the dreams of Genesis 37 indicated they would, and Joseph tested them with the threat of imprisoning one of their brothers to see how the others would react. And the text says: "They said to one another, 'Surely we are being punished because of our brother. *We saw how distressed he was when he pleaded with us for his life, but we would not listen;* that's why this distress has come upon us'" (Gen. 42:21, emphasis added).

Now let me get this straight. They threw Joseph into a cistern, then sat down to have lunch, and all the while Joseph was a few feet away crying out for his life.

"Could you pass the salt?"

"Pass the what? I can't hear you over all the pleading and crying coming from the cistern. Somebody go tell him to shut up. He's disturbing my lunch!"

Now, when they had done *that*, faking his death for their father seems small potatoes. It was the calluses. And can I say this? When you and I can no longer hear the cries of the afflicted, you and I need to get our hearts checked for calluses. If the honest tears of our own family no longer speak to our hearts, then something has gone terribly wrong.

Well, we come back from commercial and the soap opera of Genesis 37 continues, only it gets worse, if you can imagine it. Notice how the brothers asked Jacob to check out the robe and see if it was Joseph's. Talk about insincerity. Everybody knew it was Joseph's robe. It was one of a kind. I mean, they saw him wearing it every day. And they hated him for wearing it. It takes guts to be that disingenuous. And do notice that they couldn't refer to Joseph by name. They even called him "your son," not "our brother." In their guilt, they were trying to distance themselves from their own sinful act.

> When you and I can no longer hear the cries of the afflicted, you and I need to get our hearts checked for calluses.

And then they watched their own father fall apart from grief . . . grief over *their* lie! They tortured him with false news and watched Jacob convulse with sorrow and torment. Notice verse 35 says, "All his sons and daughters came to comfort him, but he refused to be comforted." He was dying a thousand deaths right in front of them, and no one would come clean and tell him the truth. The sons added another layer of shame to their deceit. Their comfort is about as sincere as the "Have a nice day" you hear as you leave the drive-through.

They should have been ashamed, but they were in too deep to notice how appalling their behavior was. Seeing the picture of an inconsolable Jacob teaches us that false comfort doesn't comfort, does it? Artificial caring counts for nothing. What Judah and his brothers offered by way of comfort just could not comfort. The non-genuine, soap-opera life is of no help to anyone.

Meanwhile, Joseph was on his way down to Egypt. And envy and jealousy sent him there. Sin will always have its way. Sinful thoughts (his brothers' hatred) lead to sinful plans (to kill him), which lead to sinful actions (selling him into the living death of slavery).

The sin of envy doesn't seem that big a deal in the early verses of chapter 37. The brothers may have thought that they'd be finished with envy, but the sin of envy isn't quite finished with them yet. Sin is centripetal in its effect. Centrifugal force pushes you to the outside. Centripetal force does the opposite: it draws you in. And the sin of envy does its work: it picks you up on the outside and draws you into its dark center.

> False comfort doesn't comfort, does it? Artificial caring counts for nothing.

Disliking your brother is small-stuff sin. It's at the outer edges of sin's effect. You'd never think of killing him. But later, deeper into the spin, you'd do just about anything. Including torturing the heart of your own father with what you know to be a lie.

In your family system and relationships, where did sin first pick you up? When we hear some of the horror stories of families, we wonder how on earth people can do certain things. And then we think, *Oh yeah; I know.* Sin began out on some softly bruised edge and, over time, became a bleeding, bitter conflict.

Friend, if you find yourself in the middle of a centripetal spin, only genuine forgiveness can get you out. There is real life work to be done. It is called forgiveness, and God will honor it and empower it. For God knows only He alone can deliver people from the kind of family cruelty that would torture the heart of a needlessly grieving father.

Our hesitation to do the work of forgiveness is often because it means life is going to get messy before it gets cleaned up. It is similar to Barbara Brown Taylor's comment on imagination in *The Preaching Life.* Just as imagination needs to be brought into order, when real forgiveness comes home and empties out its pockets, "of course, there will be some sorting to do."[5]

Real forgiveness is seldom neat or tidy or even instant, which, by cultural habit, is what we want forgiveness to be. We want to turn the page as quick as we can. We want to push Delete and have the past vanish. That's a faint hope. Reality is that trust needs to be rebuilt in some measure before that can happen. And all building takes time, not moments.

As chapter 37 ends, the bloodletting and the suffering and the pain are everywhere. It's a mess, even by the seamiest of soap-opera standards. It will take a heroic act of virtue to correct all of this. And we do find one such act near the end of the story, about eight chapters away.

But it was François Fénelon, spiritual director to the household of Louis XIV, who caught the mirrored sense of Solomon's saying that it's the little foxes that spoil the vines (Song 2:15 KJV). Fénelon wrote, "Great acts of virtue are rare because they are seldom required."[6] It is the little acts of virtue that make life work in a genuine, God-graced way.

And one of those little acts of virtue is everyday, garden-variety forgiveness one for another. So could it be that it's the little acts of virtue that keep us from requiring great ones? And could it be that some little act of virtue this week, some little forgiveness, will keep your life or my life from enduring the soap-opera pain of Genesis 37? I think you know that answer.

4

All the Right Choices, All the Wrong Results

✦ Genesis 39:1–23 ✦

Consider it pure joy, my brothers and sisters, whenever you face trials of many kinds.

—JAMES 1:2

Opportunity may only knock once, but temptation leans on the doorbell.

—ANONYMOUS

YOU KNOW THE drill. You follow all the instructions, down to the last letter, and it doesn't work. So you start over; you do everything the manual says, and it still won't work. Computers. Cars. Programming the remote for your TV. I think we've all known the complete frustration of following all the steps correctly and not getting whatever it is to work as it's supposed to.

Especially when it is your life with God. Imagine the frustration of making the right moral choices repeatedly, of following God as best you know how, and still having it all turn out wrong. Imagine the depth of discouragement of doing everything right and having it all turn out wrong.

At thirteen your mother tells you that it's time to start praying for the man you're going to marry. And one day, while you are away at college, you meet him in church: a fine Christian boy from a fine Christian family. One year later you're engaged, and two years later you're married in your home church, the place packed with loving faces and filled with joy.

But it's only three days into the honeymoon when he hits you for the first time. He says he's sorry and that he didn't mean it and it will never happen again. But it doesn't stop. And now, it's four years later, and you're sitting in an ER with a black eye, a swollen lip, and three cracked ribs, wondering what went wrong with your marriage. You did everything right. You followed all the Christian rules. And it turned out so wrong.

> You did everything right. You followed all the Christian rules. And it turned out so wrong.

Just as it did for Joseph, who did everything right and ended up in prison. He trusted God, made the right moral choice when tempted, and still ended up in prison. In Genesis 37, God gave him two dreams that portrayed him as a ruler. And since that time, he had been betrayed by his brothers, thrown in a pit to die, then sold into slavery in a foreign land, and now, at the end of chapter 39, he was imprisoned in that land.

Aren't you at least a bit surprised that he still trusted God, still followed Him after all that? I am. After each setback, you'd figure he'd be done with God, because trusting God wasn't going very well for him, was it? When you read Genesis 39, you discover where his trust in God got him: prison. Is this how God meant trust to work? Let's allow the text to inform our answer.

Now Joseph had been taken down to Egypt. Potiphar, an Egyptian who was one of Pharaoh's officials, the captain of the guard, bought him from the Ishmaelites who had taken him there.

The LORD was with Joseph so that he prospered, and he lived in the house of his Egyptian master. When his master saw that the LORD was with him and that the LORD gave him success in everything he did, Joseph found favor in his eyes and became his attendant. Potiphar put him in charge of his household, and he entrusted to his care everything he owned. From the time he put him in charge of his household and of all that he owned, the LORD blessed the household of the Egyptian because of Joseph. The blessing of the LORD was on everything Potiphar had, both in the house and in the field. So Potiphar left everything he had in Joseph's care; with Joseph in charge, he did not concern himself with anything except the food he ate.

Now Joseph was well-built and handsome, and after a while his master's wife took notice of Joseph and said, "Come to bed with me!"

But he refused. "With me in charge," he told her, "my master does not concern himself with anything in the house; everything he owns he has entrusted to my care. No one is greater in this house than I am. My master has withheld nothing from me except you, because you are his wife. How then could I do such a wicked thing and sin against God?" And though she spoke to Joseph day after day, he refused to go to bed with her or even be with her.

One day he went into the house to attend to his duties, and none of the household servants was inside. She caught him by his cloak and said, "Come to bed with me!" But he left his cloak in her hand and ran out of the house.

When she saw that he had left his cloak in her hand and had run out of the house, she called her household servants. "Look," she said to them, "this Hebrew has been brought to us to make sport of us! He came in here to sleep with me, but I screamed. When he heard me scream for help, he left his cloak beside me and ran out of the house."

She kept his cloak beside her until his master came home. Then she told him this story: "That Hebrew slave you brought us came to me to make sport of me. But as soon as I screamed for help, he left his cloak beside me and ran out of the house."

When his master heard the story his wife told him, saying, "This is how your slave treated me," he burned with anger. Joseph's master took him and put him in prison, the place where the king's prisoners were confined.

But while Joseph was there in the prison, the LORD was with him; he showed him kindness and granted him favor in the eyes of the prison warden. So the warden put Joseph in charge of all those held in the prison, and he was made responsible for all that was done there. The warden paid no attention to anything under Joseph's care, because the LORD was with Joseph and gave him success in whatever he did. (Gen. 39:1–23)

You can do your best and things can still turn out bad. Circumstances or people that are beyond your control can undermine the good choices you've made. You do things right and life doesn't work. You follow the rules, read the manual, pay attention to the directions, and it just doesn't seem to add up as you expect.

Tell me, do you "consider it pure joy" to be tried and tested this way (James 1:2)? More often, I wonder where God is in these kinds of inequitable spiritual equations.

Well, He is with you and me in the midst of it. Five times in this chapter it gets reiterated: God was with Joseph (cf. vv. 2, 3, 5, 21, 23). Everywhere Joseph went, God went with him: to bless him and strengthen him and give him favor in the eyes of those who seemed to have control over his life.

Even when life turns out not to be what we expect, God is still with us: in the shadows, in the hard places, even in those desert times when His refreshing presence seems to be only a memory. God is with us.

If you are a child of God, know this: God does not abandon His children. In the shelter of God's sovereign power and grace, Joseph never slipped out of God's care and concern. As Romans 8:28 says, in part, "God causes all things to work together for good to those who love God" (NASB).

That scripture shows up on more dusty plaques and tired-looking needlepoint wall hangings and faded bumper stickers than just about any Bible verse you can name. But the truth and power of it have not faded or grown tired or gathered dust to the point of obscurity.

For the child of God, Romans 8:28 still applies: God *does* cause all things to work together for good! And the life of Joseph reminds us today, as fresh as our morning coffee, that God does not betray the trust of His children or abandon them in hard places. He is at work in our lives even when we cannot sense His presence. He is writing out the lines of our story even when we cannot trace His hand.

As I observe kingdom life these days, it seems to me that when it comes to trusting God, doing the truth, making the choices that honor Him and honor His Word, we tend to be looking for a spiritual Tylenol effect. We want immediate results, so that if we trust God today, then by tomorrow, all we contend with will vanish. And when that doesn't happen, we think, *Well, so much for trusting God.*

The monk turned poet Kilian McDonnell, OSB, spoke for most of us, I think, when he interacted with a fragment from the Wisdom of Sirach 11:22, "Quickly God causes his blessing to flourish" (RSV). McDonnell wrote poetically and prophetically in a poem from his book of the same name,

"Swift, Lord, You Are Not": "This is not my experience. You are not God at the ready."[1]

Do you find God to be swift? I know I don't. In fact, I have found that trusting God seldom runs on my timetable. Trusting God is rarely easy or convenient. It is more like Peter in John 21, where the will of God for him was to have his hands bound and taken where he did not wish to go. Joseph was learning that as well.

In the current Christian cultural climate, we tend to judge the value of trusting God by immediate results rather than ultimate or cumulative results. Joseph trusted God and spent thirteen years in one of two conditions: as a slave or as a prisoner. Thirteen years. Building a life of faith is the work of a lifetime of trust. And it is over a lifetime that the fruit of trusting God emerges. It accumulates . . . it doesn't always come all at once or in one profound moment of experience. Could it be that we would find it easier to trust God if we took Him off the timeline of our expectations? The apostle Peter wrote that God exalts His people *in due time* (1 Peter 5:6) . . . and I've come to discover, as Joseph did, that due time is His time, not my time.

> Could it be that we would find it easier to trust God if we took Him off the timeline of our expectations?

Do take note of this: we have to be careful not to discount the measure of trust Joseph had in God just because we know how the story ends. We can turn a few pages and find him as the prime minister of Egypt, and we think, *Well, it was easy for him trust God; he ends up in a palace.*

But for all he knew at the time, his story in Genesis was coming to a sudden halt. If you listen closely to the text after verse 20, you just might hear the sound of hope falling on its face. Joseph had done the thing God would want him to do, and trusted Him for a good outcome as a result, and he found himself in prison. For all he knew, he was there for good.

He couldn't see what was on the next page or in the next chapter in the story of his life any more than you or I can see what is on the next page or the next chapter of ours. He had to trust that the One who holds the book of his life knew what He was doing as the story unfolded. And that was a very big step of trust based on very little evidence.

What evidence did Joseph have to base his trust in God upon? Well, he had the example of his father, Jacob, the deceiver. Some example of godly trust he was. He was a manipulative schemer who created a world of dysfunction and trouble for his family.

Then there was the story his father would have told him about God and the promise of making Jacob's tribe into a great nation. Do Joseph's brothers look like great nation-building material to you? Not much of a nation so far, is it? Not much of a source for hope and trust in that bunch.

Add to that his two dreams he had as a teenage boy that seemed to be saying to him that God was going to make him a ruler someday. Well, when you've been a slave in Egypt for eleven years, such dreams seem more like pipe dreams.

And that's about it. When it came to evidence for trusting God, he didn't have much to go on. I am in constant wonder at the strength of his faithful trust in God.

What evidence do we have that we ought to trust God in the choices we make? Well, we've got the Bible for a start: the written record of hundreds and hundreds of fulfilled prophecies, answered prayers, and kept promises. We have the divine record of God's faithfulness and watchfulness, His mighty redeeming acts in human and personal history, His power and justice, His grace and kindness, His mercy and love, His compassion and concern.

We have human models of trust who have walked with us and before us that are so much better than Jacob. We not only have a man like Joseph, but we have generations of godly women and men whose lives inspire us to trust God as they did. Then we have two thousand years of church history of seeing trust in God vindicated time and again.

And for the believing Christian, we have our own clear personal experience of being born again and transformed by God in response to trusting Him at salvation. And we have the indwelling Holy Spirit, God within us: not just with us in some remote, unseeable way but the very God who actually made us is living right within us. It makes me wonder how it is that we keep putting God on trial again and again, unsure if we should trust Him.

Despite having all that evidence to build trust from, some sparkling temptation will stroll by our hearts and the internal debate begins: Am I going to trust God and *do the truth*, or follow my default impulses and indulge the shadow side of my nature? Three steps forward, two steps back; inching our way forward instead of walking in step with the Spirit and bounding our way forward. And we wonder why Christian terms such as "victory" or "power" seem so clichéd and hollow to us at times.

I think this sort of disillusionment with trusting God comes when we buy into our culture's broken moral premise that immediate gratification is of higher value than long-term fulfillment. And not just a higher value, but a right. I am entitled to it. In essence, my needs, whatever they are, become my rights. With a moral compass like that, is it any wonder we are so often lost and adrift?

> Am I going to trust God and *do the truth*, or follow my default impulses and indulge the shadow side of my nature?

Can you imagine how the Bible would read if Joseph had thought that his needs were his rights? If he had made the wrong choice and had intimate relations with Potiphar's wife, he would have lost his intimacy with God. Forever a slave in Potiphar's house, toyed with like a pawn in a game by a manipulative woman, he would have exchanged his servanthood of God for slavery to her.

Then there would be no becoming a ruler, no saving of his family, no preservation of God's people. The dreams God gave him for his life would have died. And God would have to find himself another Joseph. When we make our needs our rights, we might get what we want but might very well lose our best dreams, and perhaps lose them forever.

If you watch life in our world at all, you find that like Jacob's brother, Esau, people commonly sell their future for a bowl of stew . . . or like Jack of beanstalk fame, who sold his future for a handful of magic beans. It's a story line that repeats itself every day in the headlines.

For our life stories to read differently than that, like Joseph did, we have to trust that the One who holds the book of our life knows what He is doing and where the story is headed, even when it is unclear to us how the narrative will play out. Even when life seems to be turned on its head, against all conventional wisdom we must trust Him. It's called trust. And trust is at the very heart of chapter 39.

> When we make our needs our rights, we might get what we want but might very well lose our best dreams, and perhaps lose them forever.

Now, if chapter 37 read like a soap opera, only chapter 39 can rival it. Can you hear the announcer's voice in the background, hyping a four-part miniseries on your favorite network? In a sonorous voice like that of James Earl Jones, we hear . . .

He was the handsome slave she could never own. She was the sensual woman whom no man had ever really loved. Caught in a web of intrigue, passion, and betrayal, theirs was a scandal that divided a household and changed a nation!

For most of the eleven years Joseph was a slave in the household, Potiphar's wife brazenly pursued him. There was nothing coy or delicate or subtle or seductive about it. Just bold, unvarnished sin. As the old anonymous quote has it, "Opportunity may only knock once, but temptation leans on the doorbell."

But Joseph stood his ground. He knew he should not break trust with Potiphar. But more important, he knew that he should not break trust with God. Notice in verse 9 how he expressed his muscular resolve and where his unbending trust lay at the same time: "How then could I do such a wicked thing and sin against God?"

> Our sin is always primarily against God and secondarily against the person we sin against.

In saying this, Joseph reminded all of us that our sin is always primarily against God and secondarily against the person we sin against. What did David say in Psalm 51:4? "Against you, you only, have I sinned and done what is evil in your sight."

This removes all room for rationalizing our sins: such as, "Potiphar will never know; his wife is a needy woman; I'm just meeting a basic human need in myself." If sin is primarily against God, all our rationalizations for sin fall short. Circumstances change, but God does not. That means there is little that is relative or conditional about sin. Sin is usually pretty clear-cut.

Joseph had done his best over the years to avoid getting caught in a situation of maximum temptation, maximum opportunity, and minimum resistance. Add those up and they equal a moral disaster. But despite Joseph's best efforts to avoid his master's wife, she forced the issue. She grabbed him by the cloak and he ran out in his underwear.

Well, as the old saying goes, "Hell hath no fury like a woman scorned."[2] And Potiphar's wife proved the adage true. She framed Joseph using his cloak, and accused him of attempted rape at the worst, attempted adultery at the least.

Now, the laws of Egyptian antiquity state that the sentence in that day for rape or attempted rape was death; for adultery or attempted adultery, it was being beaten a thousand times with a wooden rod: essentially the same thing as death. Few, if any, survived the beating.

But Joseph was neither put to death nor beaten. And the reason why is rooted in trust: Joseph's trust in God and Potiphar's trust in Joseph.

Our strongest relationships in life are always built on trust. Not on performance or status or money or gifts. It is why Friedrich Nietzsche is believed to have said of a friend who lied to him, "I'm not upset that you lied to me; I'm upset that from now on I can't believe you." Trust is the currency of any sound relationship, and Potiphar trusted Joseph. He learned to trust Joseph as he watched how Joseph's trust in God was rewarded with accumulated favor. When you read verses 3–6 of Genesis 39, you cannot help but notice that Joseph's trust in God and all it produced in his character—integrity, loyalty, trust, honor—were what made Joseph so trustworthy to Potiphar.

> Our strongest relationships in life are always built on trust.

All he owned he entrusted to Joseph's care. Think about that. Joseph had the keys to the chariot, the bank account numbers, all the Internet passwords, the run of the household. Essentially, Potiphar was giving the running of his life to this Hebrew slave. Now, that's trust.

And for upward of eleven years, that trust built a deeper and deeper relationship between Joseph and Potiphar. So much so that when the accusation of attempted adultery was made, Potiphar was angry, but he was unconvinced and uncertain, and he had his suspicions. He knew his wife, perhaps all too well. He knew where her passions lay and what her character was like. Could it be that Joseph wasn't the first slave she had sought after?

But still, there was his public reputation to protect. The scandal of this accusation alone would be damaging. So what could he do? He knew Joseph and trusted him. He trusted Joseph's moral character more than his own wife's word. He just couldn't bring himself to fully buy his wife's story.

Potiphar banished Joseph from his household to save face with his wife and community, but he could have had him put to death. Instead Joseph ended up not in some common prison, where one was left to rot, but in the king's prison, with the white-collar criminals. In fact, as Genesis 40:3 points out, it was the prison that Potiphar controlled and commanded.

This would be the equivalent of being in jail with the Wall Street crew who defrauded all of us, and given the not-so-hard time of cleaning flower beds, watching HBO, and playing backgammon. But perhaps more important for Potiphar, it seemed he wanted to keep Joseph within his relational reach. He put Joseph in a place where their paths were sure to cross. If so, it speaks even more of how deeply he trusted and admired Joseph.

It was Solomon who said, "Whoever walks in integrity walks securely" (Prov. 10:9). When you walk with committed trust in God, He has your back. He preserves both you and your reputation. You can count on that. Joseph did, and his life and reputation were preserved.

> Because of his unfailing trust in God, Joseph's best dreams for life are still available to him.

If you have trusted God and it seems to have backfired, if you find yourself in a hard place, if you did everything right but it seems to have turned out wrong, know this: God has your back. He will preserve your reputation and keep your life. He will watch over you and give you favor in the unlikeliest of circumstances and with the unlikeliest of people. Even in what feels like a prison. Even in the presence of your jailer.

Joseph did everything right and still ended up in prison. He trusted God by doing what he knew to be true and right and he still ended up where he didn't deserve to be. And I can make light of the king's prison, but a prison is still a prison: no freedom, no autonomy, no future . . . just yesterday happening over and over again.

But even there, the text tells us that God was with him. And God gave him favor in the eyes of the warden. It seemed that the person who trusted God was noticed by others and ended up being trusted by them. As much as a man can prosper in prison, Joseph prospered.

Because of his unfailing trust in God, Joseph's best dreams for life, given by God, were still available to him. By living out his trust in God, the dreams God gave him were not lost. They were still in play. His last chapters had not yet been written.

And neither have yours. By God's grace and goodness, there are plans that God still has in store for you. If we abandon our trust in God in the midst of test and trial, we are throwing away our best future, the one He has planned for us. Don't stop one trust too soon. Could it be that the future you've always longed for is the thing you lose by giving up on God one trust too soon?

> When you walk with committed trust in God, He has your back. He preserves both you and your reputation.

For Joseph, there was no exaltation to prime minister without enduring the tests and trial of this temptation. What might we lose if we do not trust God and endure the test or trial of some temptation? Another shopworn Scripture verse that, though threadbare from overuse, has never lost its meaning or its power: "'For I know the plans I have for you,' declares the LORD, 'plans to prosper you and not to harm you, plans to give you hope and a future'" (Jer. 29:11). To keep that promise in play, we must trust God in the midst of all that tries us. Trusting God keeps all of life's best and God's best possibilities in play for you and me.

I have an old friend who commonly asks me when a big decision is at hand: "Do we trust God or do we just *say* we trust God?" Tough question. But let's trust the God who has written us into the narrative that is His story, that what He intends to write with our lives as we trust Him is the kind of stuff that God-given dreams are made of and made for. Could it be that if we did, we'd find ourselves strangely blessed in the corridors of the prime minister's palace?

5

When a Dream Dies

✦ Genesis 40:1–23 ✦

Much dreaming and many words are meaningless.
Therefore fear God.

—ECCLESIASTES 5:7

I'm sick of following my dreams. I'm just going to ask
them where they're going and hook up with them later.

—MITCH HEDBERG, COMEDIAN

SOMEONE ONCE SAID that if you have a recurring dream, it means you haven't gotten the message. I know that feeling. My recurring dream is that I am about to preach and I cannot find my notes. I've left them in my office. The problem is that I am standing behind this big pulpit in my pajamas. I need everyone to bow their heads and have someone else lead out in a long prayer so I can run back to my office, find my notes, get dressed properly, and come back just in time to say amen and preach. Wouldn't Freud have had fun with me?

We all dream, of course. Not always your standard insecurity dream, like mine, but we all dream. And no matter

56

how plodding or unimaginative, how fierce or terrifying, how poetic or pedestrian our dreams may be, there may be something being said to us that is worth listening to. And we all want to know what a dream we've had means, don't we?

And that's the rub. In a world full of pseudo Freuds and serious frauds, fortune-tellers and phonies, earnest seekers and honest scholars, that's a hard thing to sort out.

For me, dreams are not an area of compelling interest. I tend to take a rather simple, nonmystical approach to them. For example, when I see a familiar face in a dream, I wake myself up and pray for that person. I take his or her appearance in my dream as God prompting me to pray for the individual.

Still, I would say there are at least a few things we can say about dreams. We spend a third of our life in a world that is as real to us while we are in it as the world of waking reality. And while we

> There may be something being said to us that is worth listening to.

are in that other world, at a minimum, it has something to say about who we are and where we have been and what we long to be.

And a second thing: in dreams we learn that our lives are a great deal richer and deeper . . . more intricately related, more mysterious and complex than we commonly suppose. And that's worth paying attention to.

I believe that God can still speak in dreams today. It is not His primary means of communication with us, of course. And what He is saying is seldom, if ever, literal. And He says nothing that would contradict the revelation of Scripture or the character of Jesus Christ.

But there are sound Christian scholars who have written a lot about dreams and finding God's voice in them. Gene Edwards, in *A Tale of Three Kings*, wrote that only God knows the future, and He's not telling. Well, maybe in dreams He whispers.

In the life of Joseph, everything was held together by the most fragile of dreams. A teenage boy's dreams. Two dreams where he was pictured as ruling over his family. And his whole story was shaped by the fulfilling of those two dreams.

> Only God knows the future and He's not telling. Well, maybe in dreams He whispers.

At the beginning of chapter 40, it looked as though those two dreams were never going to be fulfilled. Joseph was unjustly in prison, and as far as he knew, he was in there for good. Think about that. He had no idea how long or what the final sentence would be. But two more dreams began to change all that.

Some time later, the cupbearer and the baker of the king of Egypt offended their master, the king of Egypt. Pharaoh was angry with his two officials, the chief cupbearer and the chief baker, and put them in custody in the house of the captain of the guard, in the same prison where Joseph was confined. The captain of the guard assigned them to Joseph, and he attended them.

After they had been in custody for some time, each of the two men—the cupbearer and the baker of the king of Egypt, who were being held in prison— had a dream the same night, and each dream had a meaning of its own.

When Joseph came to them the next morning, he saw that they were dejected. So he asked Pharaoh's officials who were in custody with him in his master's house, "Why do you look so sad today?"

"We both had dreams," they answered, "but there is no one to interpret them."

Then Joseph said to them, "Do not interpretations belong to God? Tell me your dreams."

So the chief cupbearer told Joseph his dream. He said to him, "In my dream I saw a vine in front of me, and on the vine were three branches. As soon as it budded, it blossomed, and its clusters ripened into grapes. Pharaoh's cup was in my hand, and I took the grapes, squeezed them into Pharaoh's cup and put the cup in his hand."

"This is what it means," Joseph said to him. "The three branches are three days. Within three days Pharaoh will lift up your head and restore you to your position, and you will put Pharaoh's cup in his hand, just as you used to do when you were his cupbearer. But when all goes well with you, remember me and show me kindness; mention me to Pharaoh and get me out of this prison. I was forcibly carried off from the land of the Hebrews, and even here I have done nothing to deserve being put in a dungeon."

When the chief baker saw that Joseph had given a favorable interpretation, he said to Joseph, "I too had a dream: On my head were three baskets of bread. In the top basket were all kinds of baked goods for Pharaoh, but the birds were eating them out of the basket on my head."

"This is what it means," Joseph said. "The three baskets are three days. Within three days Pharaoh will lift off your head and impale your body on a pole. And the birds will eat away your flesh."

Now the third day was Pharaoh's birthday, and he gave a feast for all his officials. He lifted up the heads of the chief cupbearer and the chief baker in the presence of his officials: He restored the chief cupbearer to his position, so that he once again put the cup into Pharaoh's hand—but he impaled the chief baker, just as Joseph had said to them in his interpretation.

> The chief cupbearer, however, did not remember
> Joseph; he forgot him. (Gen. 40:1–23)

Was God being fair in this account? Joseph's non-God-fearing cellmates had their dreams realized right on schedule, while Joseph was still twisting in the wind with his. Was God toying with Joseph? Shouldn't He have been rewarding him for the integrity and purity he displayed in the incident with Potiphar's wife?

There had been an assumption at play all along in this account of Joseph's life that Joseph was going to end up a powerful ruler someday. In part, that's because we know how the story ends. Or at the very least, we can look ahead in our Bibles and see that it does, in fact, end that way.

That assumption turned mostly on the interpretation given to Joseph's early dreams by his brothers and his father in chapter 37. They are the ones who said, "Will we actually come and bow down to you?" That's where the whole idea of Joseph ruling over his family began.

But all of that was looking unlikely to happen when Joseph was in prison with no idea of how long the sentence was going to last. It was all very disillusioning. His status as the favored son of Jacob was no help in seeing those early dreams fulfilled. Potiphar, who was so highly placed in Pharaoh's court, was certainly no help. In fact, he made things worse. It seemed all the people and circumstances in Joseph's life that he might have placed confidence in for seeing those dreams fulfilled had proved fruitless.

> The interpretation of Joseph's dreams belonged to God and God alone.

When the cupbearer and the baker had dreams, notice what Joseph said in Genesis 40:8: "Do not interpretations belong to God?" The interpretations of Joseph's two dreams did not belong to his brothers or his father or Freud or some fraudulent gypsy at a summer county fair. They belonged to God.

The interpretation of Joseph's dreams belonged to God and God alone. Can't you hear him in that prison? "I used to think that anybody could figure out a dream. I used to think my brothers were right, and look where it landed me. I used to think that I had this big future coming my way. I used to think . . ."

Friends, I think it was through all the humbling experiences Joseph had endured to date and was still enduring in the present tense of Genesis 40 that he figured something out. Dream interpretations belong to the God who knows the future, not human amateurs who can only guess.

> [Ultimate trust] means trusting God in the dark, not just in the light. In hard places, not just when it's convenient.

He was no longer banking his future on how his family understood and interpreted his youthful dreams. I think he was long past that. Real life had seen to that. All that he had confidence in had been stripped away. His only confidence left was in God. It took a lot to get him to that place, but he finally knew that God was all he had.

He then came to the place of ultimate trust. And he knew it. Do you? Do I? Do we know it when God has stripped away everything in which we have placed our confidence for seeing His dreams realized for our lives? Because Joseph knew, and the Bible would have us know, that when it all comes down, it all comes down to trusting God: no plan B, no second guesses, no back door.

And what does that kind of trust look like? It means trusting God in the dark, not just in the light. Trusting God in hard places, not just when it's convenient.

In Psalm 105 we read about the imprisonment of Joseph in Egypt and how it was all part of what God had in mind to preserve His people. In that psalm, God says He sent a famine on the land of promise, the land of Canaan, as a means of weakening the kings who might otherwise destroy Jacob and his clan while it is still being formed. And that is how Egypt became part of the divine equation. It reads, "And *he sent a man before them—Joseph, sold as a slave.* They bruised his feet with shackles, his neck was put in irons, till what he foretold came to pass, till the word of the LORD proved him true. The king sent and released him, the ruler of peoples set him free. He made him master of his household, ruler over all he possessed" (vv. 17–21; emphasis added).

I think we learn here that God is always thinking ahead while we most commonly think behind: Why did this happen to me? Why didn't I get my way? Why didn't it happen like I knew it was supposed to? Maybe the questions need to change. Maybe it should be: How will God make use of this in my life?

When Joseph was sold as a slave, God was actually placing him where he needed him to be in redemptive history. And when Joseph ended up in prison, God was actually positioning him for delivering His people. Could it be the hard place you find yourself in is the very place God meant for you to be for purposes you cannot quite see yet?

> His dreams for you are not simply all about you.

It is humbling to remember that in the sovereign wisdom of God, His dreams for you are not simply all about you. There was a famine coming, and God's intention was to preserve His people in the land of Egypt, which was the breadbasket of that world.

Beloved, your God-given dreams are meant to fit into a larger picture and a larger purpose: God's. They are not all about you, like some twenty-first-century mantra of self-centeredness. They are about Him and His plans for His world and your place in it.

Joseph couldn't see it at the time, and maybe we can't see it either when it happens to us. But every step Joseph took on his journey of trust brought him closer to the fulfillment of God's dreams for him, not further from them.

Every character in this remarkable story had an agenda, a purpose, and a plan they were trying to work. Pharaoh, Potiphar, Potiphar's wife, Jacob, his sons, and on and on it went. But even the crafty scheming of Potiphar's wife or the petty whim of Pharaoh could not frustrate the plans and purposes of God.

> Joseph in prison is closer to the throne of Pharaoh than ever before.

Solomon wrote, "Many are the plans of a person's heart, but it is the LORD's purpose that prevails" (Prov. 19:21). Joseph said as much to his brothers years later in Genesis 50:20: "You intended to harm me, but God intended it for good to accomplish what is now being done, the saving of many lives."

Trust in a time of trial and testing is seeing the hand of God before you can figure out what He is going to write. It is trusting Him before you get to the place of retrospect when you see how it all made sense.

When Job said he would trust God even if God were to slay him (Job 13:15 KJV), he was reminding all of us that the hard times we go through in life are not a barometer of God's love for us. God's love is not expressed in the measure of our creature comforts but within the framework of those hard-to-discern purposes.

When you trust God, even the downward steps move you forward in fulfilling His purposes and the dreams He has for your life. Even in his last setback, Joseph in prison was closer to the throne of Pharaoh than ever before. In your life and mine, who would ever have thought that a step down would equal a way forward? Could it be for any of us that the best way forward is cleverly disguised as another step down?

No downward step or setback takes you out of the reach of God. There is no dark corner of your life's experience where the blessing and favor of God cannot find you. There is no God-forsaken place in this world where God cannot show up to bless you.

Joseph's story proves the point: if God can find you in Potiphar's house, he can find you in Potiphar's prison. Even there, the favor of God on Joseph was self-evident and it created hope and possibilities for him.

> Dreams are never enough. Only God is enough.

And that favor helped hold his confidence in God intact. As the whole drama unfolded, Joseph was patiently submitting to the will of God, patiently trusting God when all he had to go on was a teenage boy's dream. But when those dreams died, when the interpretation his brothers gave them no longer seemed possible, his trust shifted to God and God alone. And the way God favored him as a result gave him hope and confidence in God.

By chapter 40, Joseph was no longer trusting in the threadbare dreams of his youth. As verses 14–15 imply, he'd be glad just to be out of prison. But while he gave up on those dreams long ago, he had not given up on God. Those early dreams were not enough . . . dreams are never enough. Only God is enough.

We don't bank our future on dreams, however intriguing they might be or however promising they appear. We trust the God who makes promises and keeps them. The God who knows and builds the future. Our trust in God for our future is not trust in the preferred, self-designed future of our expectation but in God Himself.

Joseph's father, Jacob, wrestled with God at the river Jabbok and walked with a limp for the rest of his life. Joseph watched that limp just about every day of his childhood. He knew what it meant. It was like a living sign of his father's connection to God. Joseph knew that his father, as weak and broken as he was, was still the one to whom the great promise of God had come: "All peoples on earth will be blessed through you and your offspring" (Gen. 28:14).

As God responded to Joseph's prison-days trust, He did not offer a Get Out of Jail Free card: He gave Joseph His favor. Potiphar was blessed through Joseph. The prison warden was blessed through Joseph.

It must certainly have begun to dawn on Joseph that all that blessing was God staying faithful to that old promise made to his father and his grandfather. And then to him. God's faithfulness to His promises makes trust possible even in the hardest of places.

Could it be that we are meant to trust our journey with God as a whole, not simply base our trust in God upon the circumstances of a particular day or struggles of a particular season that we do not understand? Are we meant to trust that God knows what is coming for us when we can't see what tomorrow holds? And if He knows, and we are His, isn't that is enough? And we'll be all right? I think so.

> God's faithfulness to His promises makes trust possible even in the hardest of places.

6

When God Falls Silent
✦ Genesis 41:1–40 ✦

The chief cupbearer, however, did not remember Joseph; he forgot him.

—Genesis 40:23

We must be willing to get rid of the life we've planned, so as to have the life that is waiting for us.

—Attributed to Joseph Campbell

REAL HUMAN LIFE is full of awkward silences. Cell phone conversations that stutter and stammer along. Forgetting the name of the person to whom you are speaking, mid-sentence. Being at a loss for words when a word is most needed. We all know the clumsy awkwardness of silence.

Well, there was an awkward silence in the story of Joseph. And truth be told, it was God's awkward silence. In the small, blank space between the end of Genesis 40 and the beginning of chapter 41, there was a world of silent waiting for an implied promise to be kept. Then finally, in chapter 41, God's will got loud.

When two full years had passed, Pharaoh had a
dream: He was standing by the Nile, when out of
the river there came up seven cows, sleek and fat,
and they grazed among the reeds. After them, seven
other cows, ugly and gaunt, came up out of the Nile
and stood beside those on the riverbank. And the
cows that were ugly and gaunt ate up the seven sleek,
fat cows. Then Pharaoh woke up.

He fell asleep again and had a second dream:
Seven heads of grain, healthy and good, were
growing on a single stalk. After them, seven other
heads of grain sprouted—thin and scorched by the
east wind. The thin heads of grain swallowed up the
seven healthy, full heads. Then Pharaoh woke up; it
had been a dream.

In the morning his mind was troubled, so he sent
for all the magicians and wise men of Egypt. Pharaoh
told them his dreams, but no one could interpret
them for him.

Then the chief cupbearer said to Pharaoh, "Today
I am reminded of my shortcomings. Pharaoh was
once angry with his servants, and he imprisoned me
and the chief baker in the house of the captain of
the guard. Each of us had a dream the same night,
and each dream had a meaning of its own. Now a
young Hebrew was there with us, a servant of the
captain of the guard. We told him our dreams, and he
interpreted them for us, giving each man the interpretation of his dream. And things turned out exactly
as he interpreted them to us: I was restored to my
position, and the other man was impaled."

So Pharaoh sent for Joseph, and he was quickly
brought from the dungeon. When he had shaved and
changed his clothes, he came before Pharaoh.

Pharaoh said to Joseph, "I had a dream, and no one can interpret it. But I have heard it said of you that when you hear a dream you can interpret it."

"I cannot do it," Joseph replied to Pharaoh, "but God will give Pharaoh the answer he desires."

Then Pharaoh said to Joseph, "In my dream I was standing on the bank of the Nile, when out of the river there came up seven cows, fat and sleek, and they grazed among the reeds. After them, seven other cows came up—scrawny and very ugly and lean. I had never seen such ugly cows in all the land of Egypt. The lean, ugly cows ate up the seven fat cows that came up first. But even after they ate them, no one could tell that they had done so; they looked just as ugly as before. Then I woke up.

"In my dream I saw seven heads of grain, full and good, growing on a single stalk. After them, seven other heads sprouted—withered and thin and scorched by the east wind. The thin heads of grain swallowed up the seven good heads. I told this to the magicians, but none of them could explain it to me."

Then Joseph said to Pharaoh, "The dreams of Pharaoh are one and the same. God has revealed to Pharaoh what he is about to do. The seven good cows are seven years, and the seven good heads of grain are seven years; it is one and the same dream. The seven lean, ugly cows that came up afterward are seven years, and so are the seven worthless heads of grain scorched by the east wind: They are seven years of famine.

"It is just as I said to Pharaoh: God has shown Pharaoh what he is about to do. Seven years of great abundance are coming throughout the land of Egypt, but seven years of famine will follow them. Then all the abundance in Egypt will be forgotten, and the famine will ravage the land. The abundance in the land will not be remembered, because the famine that follows it will be so severe. The reason the dream was given to Pharaoh in two forms is that the matter has been firmly decided by God, and God will do it soon.

"And now let Pharaoh look for a discerning and wise man and put him in charge of the land of Egypt. Let Pharaoh appoint commissioners over the land to take a fifth of the harvest of Egypt during the seven years of abundance. They should collect all the food of these good years that are coming and store up the grain under the authority of Pharaoh, to be kept in the cities for food. This food should be held in reserve for the country, to be used during the seven years of famine that will come upon Egypt, so that the country may not be ruined by the famine."

The plan seemed good to Pharaoh and to all his officials. So Pharaoh asked them, "Can we find anyone like this man, one in whom is the spirit of God?"

Then Pharaoh said to Joseph, "Since God has made all this known to you, there is no one so discerning and wise as you. You shall be in charge of my palace, and all my people are to submit to your orders. Only with respect to the throne will I be greater than you." (Gen. 41:1–40)

At the end of chapter 40, Joseph and the cupbearer made a deal. After Joseph interpreted the cupbearer's dream, he asked the cupbearer when he got out in three days to mention him to Pharaoh and get him out of prison, where he was being held unjustly.

Although it goes unsaid, the circumstances and the story line implied the promise: the cupbearer was going to put in a good word for Joseph with Pharaoh, and Joseph was surely going to be helped out of his unjust prison sentence.

The cupbearer got out in three days just as Joseph said he would, but Joseph lived for two more years in the awkward silence of God that dwelt between Genesis 40:23 and 41:1. "The chief cupbearer . . . forgot him." Solomon wrote, "Like a bad tooth and an unsteady foot is confidence in a faithless man in time of trouble" (Prov. 25:19 NASB).

The thing about Joseph's prison sentence was that it was indefinite. It had no end point, no release date. For all he knew, it would be forever. In some sense it was like grief in the human soul or a lover's broken heart: you wonder when the pain of it will finally be over but there is no timetable for it. It feels as though it will go on forever. And if you were Joseph, that prison could very well have been forever.

In Genesis 40:1, we are told that Joseph was already in prison for some time before all the events of the dream interpretation for the cupbearer and baker happened. Chapter 41 begins by saying that two full years more passed before anything began to stir in the story of Joseph, an eternity when one is in prison.

All there was, was waiting. With each passing day, if you listen closely to the emptiness between chapters 40 and 41, you could hear the sound of hope falling flat on its face. Every time the key turned in the lock, Joseph's heart would jump at the thought that there was news of his release, only to have his heart broken again. Time crawled and all hope retreated with every shadow that crept up the wall of his cell.

> If you listen closely to the emptiness between chapters 40 and 41, you can hear the sound of hope falling flat on its face.

Waiting like that is real suffering. But you know that. You know about waiting. Waiting for the lab results to come back. Waiting for a callback on a job. Waiting for a cloud of depression to lift. Waiting for the long night to be over. Waiting for a page to turn, an illness to pass, a change to finally come. Waiting for a friend to call you friend again. Just waiting. Waiting in the awkward silence of God.

At such times the temptation is to just give up. The weight of disappointed hope just falls through the floor of your soul which has been weakened by the dry rot of waiting. Emily Dickinson wrote:

A great Hope fell
You heard no noise
The Ruin was within
Oh cunning Wreck
That told no Tale
And let no Witness in.[1]

Recently, while reading William Barker's book *A Savior for All Seasons,* I was reminded of an event from my childhood that I would rather not have remembered.

I was about five or six years old, and the county fair was set up in a grocery store parking lot not that far from our neighborhood. One muggy, late-summer night, my folks took us four kids just to get us out of the house and let the air conditioner have a rest.

> The weight of disappointed hope just falls through the floor of your soul that has been weakened by the dry rot of waiting.

Not long after we got there, somehow I got separated from my parents and wandered around lost for about two hours. I kept waiting, expecting to be found. I looked everywhere for my folks in what seemed to me like a vast crowd. It was all confusion, noise, bedlam, and encroaching darkness. And no one showed up.

I thought I'd head back to the car, but I couldn't find it. Then I thought I would walk home. After a few blocks, I was hopelessly lost and tried to find my way back to the fair. Night came on and my lostness only deepened. My waiting now seemed endless. Until a neighbor found me wandering down a side street and took me home, I felt completely abandoned.

Now, to a little boy, this is an experience of real suffering. Many of you would have similar stories you could tell. But real doubts began to creep into my mind, the kind William Barker reawakened and underlined in my thoughts with his book.

Maybe my parents didn't love me . . . didn't care about me. Maybe they didn't want me. Maybe they were trying to get rid of me. Why didn't they come? Were they even looking for me? Where were they when I needed them so badly?

Those were real dark moments of waiting for a five-year-old, much as prison was a dark season of waiting for Joseph. Forgotten by the cupbearer, he was left to wait. And wonder. *Why is he taking so long? Why doesn't some news come? We had a deal . . . why doesn't he keep his end of the bargain?*

If you were Joseph, you'd do everything you could to keep hope alive. After the first few days passed and your early expectations didn't hold up, you'd find yourself inventing reasonable rationalizations for the cupbearer's tardiness: he'd fallen sick; he'd gone to visit family; he was off on business for Pharaoh.

Then you would turn to marking the days and months on the wall. But the wall would just fill up with marks as the days themselves became ever more empty. Time would gnaw away at hope. Eventually, inevitably, you would resign yourself to what it is: over. And you would give up.

Only we're no longer talking about Joseph, are we? We're talking about you and what it's been like for you to live with the awkward silence of God. Some cupbearer in your life never kept his or her promise. And plenty of time has gone by and you're still in your prison. And you feel let down, disappointed, abandoned by God. You feel forgotten.

You begin to feel like John the Baptist in Matthew 11. He too was in prison. Because he was the one who baptized

Jesus, the one who saw the Spirit of God descend upon Jesus like a dove, the one who heard the very voice of God the Father speak His blessing over God the Son . . . *that* John asked through his disciples, "Are you the one who is to come, or should we expect someone else?" (Matt. 11:3). And behind that question was the reason for it. If we could hear John speak off the record of Scripture, he'd likely say, "Are You the one . . . *because what has happened to me makes me think maybe I got it wrong. Maybe You're not the one. I'm trapped in some kind of awkward silence with God, and I'm not getting any answers from Him.*"

That is when all the darker questions about God really begin to surface. And in our experience of the silence of God, we reflect John the Baptist's doubts in the questions of *our* minds. We reflect the doubts of a little boy lost in the dark maze of his waiting.

Maybe God doesn't love me . . . doesn't care about me. Maybe He doesn't want me. You are haunted not by the reality of things, but what things feel like. *Maybe God's given up on me and He's trying to get rid of me. Why doesn't He come? Is He even looking for me? Where is He when I need him so badly? Maybe He's abandoned me for some reason I cannot figure out. And maybe He's just forgotten me.*

> Could it be we learn more of Him while living out of our questions than we do living out of our answers?

Of all men born of a woman, none were greater in Jesus' estimation than John the Baptist. Yet John had questions. And Jesus answered them in the balance of Matthew 11.

It must mean that if we have questions of God, our questions don't drive Him away. In a strange way, they invite Him into our life to answer them. Could it be our honest doubts are a doorway to a closer relationship with God? Could it be we learn more of Him while living out of our questions than we do living out of our answers?

Part of the attraction to Joseph's life is that it is littered with fascinating dreams. But for all the fascinating dreams and what their interpretation might hold for us, the higher skill in life is simply interpreting life—real life—the circumstances in which we find ourselves.

Often our default interpretation of any awkward silence in life, any season of waiting, is that God has forgotten us or abandoned us . . . not kept His side of the bargain. In a high-tech world that overvalues immediacy, it's hard to see a divine purpose that could be greater than our immediate need. We would never blame Joseph for thinking such thoughts because we have thought them ourselves so many times.

But against every expectation, it appears that was not what Joseph was thinking. Joseph emerged from that season of the silence of God and we are most surprised by what is missing. He came out of prison with a number of things missing: bitterness, vengeance, anger, questions, doubts about God, you name it. It seems that during all that awkward silence of God, that period of time when all he could do was wait, Joseph questioned God but never stopped trusting Him.

Joseph didn't interpret the awkward silence of God as abandonment. He certainly gave up on trusting the cupbearer. He certainly gave up on relying on people to get him out. But apparently, he never gave up on trusting God. Perhaps he experienced firsthand what Fénelon advised, "We should never abandon ourselves to God so fully as when he seems to abandon us."[2]

It could only be his rock-solid trust in God that made the difference for Joseph. The only way to judge the impact of his time of awkward silence with God is to measure the Joseph who came out of it. And the Joseph we find described near the end of Genesis 41 was a Joseph we haven't really seen before. He was clearly wiser and more discerning than the prisoner who felt only the injustice of his circumstances in chapter 40 (cf. 40:15). Somewhere in the blank space between the two chapters, something truly transformational happened.

On the other side of the awkward silence of God was a man who was wise and discerning; humble and yet bold at the same time; supremely confident and entirely filled with God. That can only be the fruit of trusting God in the awkward silence and, at times, the painful darkness of it all. He was sold into slavery as a petulant boy and came out of slavery and prison a real man of God. And trust in God made all the difference.

We see the remarkable trust Joseph had in God in evidence in Genesis 41:15: "Pharaoh said to Joseph, 'I had a dream, and no one can interpret it. But I have heard it said of you that when you hear a dream you can interpret it.'"

Joseph had Pharaoh right where he wanted him. He had all the power and leverage any man could want. He held all the cards. He could cut a deal with Pharaoh; trade the dream interpretation for a Get Out of Jail Free card; get a new life somewhere else; get even with those who imprisoned him unjustly; you name it. It was his one shot at power. He had literally waited years for this.

But look what he did. He threw away all of his leverage and all of his power in one sentence and entrusted his future entirely to God: "'I cannot do it,' Joseph replied to Pharaoh, 'but God will give Pharaoh the answer he desires'" (41:16).

"I cannot do it." After being presented before Pharaoh as a dream interpreter, Joseph said, in effect, "Beats me! I have no idea!" But it was a much wiser Joseph then. He knew how things had worked out when he cut a deal with the cupbearer. He was basically saying, "I'm not going down that road again. I'm not going to angle life based on trusting men versus trusting God." Now, that's an enormous risk of faith and trust!

Because remember: Joseph was talking to a man who was considered a deity in his land. This Pharaoh was an Egyptian "god." The circumstances couldn't be more freighted with implications for Joseph. When he said God could solve Pharaoh's problem, he was telling this other god right to his face that Pharaoh couldn't do what God—the *only* God—could do. It was like saying, "You are supposed to be a god around here. But apparently you're not much of one 'cause if you were, you'd know the future . . . you'd know the answer to your own dreams . . . you'd know what's coming down!"

Now, that was putting it all on the line and trusting God! Joseph had long ago given up on trusting people to do for him that which only God could do. During that awkward silence of God and so much of what had come before that, all of his trust in people was stripped away.

Anyone who could ever have been an advantage in life for him, who could have protected him or delivered him, never came through for him. He wasn't sheltered by the favoritism of his father, or protected by the high-ranking influence of his master Potiphar, or freed from prison by the networking possibilities of the cupbearer. The cupbearer's forgetfulness wasn't the first time someone had disappointed him. He was getting used to it now. God was all he had.

> Joseph had long ago given up on trusting people to do for him that which God could do.

But what I think we are meant to learn is that when you've gotten past the point of trusting people to do for you that which only God can do, you lose any sense of bitterness toward people when they disappoint you. Why should you be bitter? You didn't expect them to be God for you, did you? Because if you did, you would end up bitter, and bitterness is its own prison.

I may have gotten lost trying to find my house as a kid, but as an adult I lost my house altogether. It was during the seventies that I became a believer and was almost immediately called to the ministry. The problem was that I had to sell my house to make it happen, and it was during a crippling recession, lineups at the pumps, thousands of houses on the market. We lost everything.

But the hardest part of the story was that I had a close relative who was a lawyer who told me he'd clean up the paperwork. Months later, when I was twelve hundred miles away at school, I got a letter serving me notice of legal proceedings against me over my former house. My relative had done nothing about it.

Three days later, I was on a city bus heading to school, and a young First Nations man about my age sat down beside me and struck up a conversation. He told me he worked legal aid for social services. And two days later, he made my legal problem go away. A coincidence? No, a God-incidence. Who knew God had angels who were First Nations?

I learned in that experience the disappointment that comes with misplaced trust in people and the power of trusting God. And in the learning of that, I was set free from any grudge or bitterness.

And that was what Joseph lost in prison: the bitterness we feel and often silently hold against the people who disappoint us—people who we expected could do for us that which only God can do. And with that loss of bitterness, Joseph lost the dark urge for vengeance or the anger that fueled it. He was not out for the cupbearer's head or the head of Potiphar's wife. Later we will see he's not even out for his brothers' heads. In trusting God he came to be at peace within himself.

Does this mean we should never trust people? Of course not. But it seems to me from this account that when you and I quit counting on people to deliver that which only God can give us, we are on our way to a much healthier inner life. After all, the middle verse in all the Bible says, "It is better to take refuge in the LORD than to trust in princes" (Ps. 118:9).

You and I know this. It's all been said before. But it needs to be said again because apparently, we weren't paying attention! So David repeated himself and said, "Do not put your trust in princes, in human beings, who cannot save" (Ps. 146:3).

David could have said, "Do not trust in cupbearers," because believe me: cupbearers are everywhere these days. From parents and family, to Oprah and Dr. Phil, from the latest weight-loss guru to the person at work who you hope will network a promotion for you or the guy you met at the Starbucks who said he'd put a word in for you. Princes all, cupbearers all, Joseph's brothers all.

There are countless people of status that we are counting on to get us out of prisons for which God and God alone holds the key. Read the magazine covers in the grocery stores. Our culture is counting on cupbearers all the time to set them free. To put in a good word somehow, someway, somewhere, with someone and get them out of the prison they are in.

The counsel of Scripture here is not cynical. Again, it's not that we should never trust people. It is that we should trust God first and foremost. He is to get our primary trust . . . even in those seasons of awkward silence. We are not meant to rely upon the cupbearers of this world to get us out of everything we contend with in life. There are seasons in life where only God can be relied upon. We are meant to trust God: trust that He is looking out for us, that His timing is right, that His plan is unfolding. Trust that He has not forgotten us or abandoned us.

"God has revealed to Pharaoh what he is about to do . . . God has shown Pharaoh what he is about to do . . . The matter has been firmly decided by God, and God will do it soon" (Gen. 41:25, 28, 32).

When Joseph was exalted in the land as a ruler, it was God's word and God's hand. But then look at the wisdom that came from Joseph, that was rooted in that season of the silence of God in verses 33–36. It's hard to remember that this was the precocious boy of chapter 37 who, in his un-wisdom with his brothers and father, was an unwitting cog in the machinery of his own exile.

In that season of silence, he apparently learned more about humility than simply how to spell it. His elevation to the right hand of Pharaoh was owing to God's hand and the wisdom he gained while under God's hand. Joseph didn't get the job because he was good at the secret mysteries of dream interpretation. As Pharaoh said in verses 39–40, he got the job because he was wise.

When we see him functioning out of such poise and confidence in the presence of Pharaoh, it's hard to remember that earlier that morning he was a Hebrew slave in Pharaoh's prison. But it was more than confidence. Joseph was functioning out of knowledge. His trust was not theoretical. It was rooted in his experience of the faithfulness of God while he was in Potiphar's household and when he was in prison. Five times in chapter 39 we read, "the Lord was with Joseph."

Joseph experienced the faithfulness of God and never forgot it. He was so absolutely certain of God's faithfulness that he was secure in his own skin. The fruit of trusting God was the capacity to live out of the center of who God made him to be. He went from a foolish, naive teenage boy to a man of extraordinary wisdom.

And where did Joseph get all of this wisdom? The blank space between Genesis 40:23 and 41:1. From that time of the awkward silence of God. As I said earlier, the only way to judge the impact of his time of awkward silence with God is to measure the Joseph who came out of it. And the Joseph we find here in chapter 41 is the Joseph that the blank space between the two chapters created.

In a very real sense, Joseph was a picture of the handiwork of God. Pharaoh said there was no one like Joseph for wisdom and discernment. And all it took to get him there was betrayal by his brothers, being sold into slavery, and being unjustly thrown into prison and forgotten.

Can I ask the question, then, that the story begs? Who are you and I becoming in our season of the awkward silence of God? Or who have we become now that we have gone through them? A lot of people have a story of disappointment to tell. And you can read between every line the feelings of bitterness, anger, and the hunger for vengeance. Such encounters suggest that we don't always handle the awkward silence of God very well. An anonymous poet wrote:

> When God wants to drill a man,
> And thrill a man,
> And skill a man
> When God wants to mold a man
> To play the noblest part;
>
> When He yearns with all His heart
> To create so great and bold a man
> That all the world might be amazed,
> Watch His methods, watch His ways!
>
> How He ruthlessly perfects
> Whom He royally elects!
> How He hammers him and hurts him,
> And with mighty blows converts him
>
> Into trial shapes of clay which
> Only God understands;
> While his tortured heart is crying
> And he lifts beseeching hands.
>
> How He bends but never breaks
> When his good He undertakes;
> How He uses whom He chooses,
> And which every purpose fuses him;
> By every act induces him,
> To try His splendor out—
> God knows what He's about!

And that is what trust in God asks of us: we trust that He knows what He's about, that He knows what He's doing, when the silences are indeed awkward and we feel forgotten or abandoned by Him.

We all want God to work faster, but apparently the timing of God includes the forgetfulness of cupbearers. Could it be that among the things that God factors into His plans for you are the forgetfulness of your cupbearers and the time needed to shape you into the person He can best use?

Life really *is* full of awkward silences. They are bewildering as well as clumsy. Don't be persuaded by the naively spiritually certain, with their Sunday school answers that God paints only in black and white. There are a lot of gray tones in sorting out this journey with Him. There are days when trying to figure out what God is up to in your life can seem as awkward as trying to tie your shoes with boxing gloves on. Yet it is important to remember that while you wait, your waiting is not wasted. God is at work. He hasn't forgotten or abandoned you.

> Could it be that among the things that God factors into His plans for you are the forgetfulness of your cupbearers and the time needed to shape you into the person He can best use?

I live in a small town in Kentucky near Lexington, where I serve First Alliance Church. Recently I saw a car, driving down the main street of our town, that was hardly a car. It was so beat up and rusted out that you could see the engine block through the fenders. But you couldn't see through the windshield because it was as cracked as eggs at breakfast. And you couldn't tell what the original color was because the rust had been painted over so many times.

We've all seen this kind of car before: one door is blue and held on by a bungee cord. The other doors are light green and held in place by a prayer. However, like all such cars, the one

I saw had one thing that worked: the sound system. It was so loud that folks were dancing to it three counties over. The driver's got a thousand-dollar sound system in a ten-cent car.

But it was the back of the car that told the real story behind the story. There, on the back bumper, was a sticker that read, "This is not an abandoned car." Now, that's a faith statement if I've ever heard one! By every appearance it had been given up on long ago. But it mattered to somebody, and it was still on the road.

Take a good look at the space between Genesis 40 and 41. There was a Hebrew slave in an Egyptian prison who by every appearance had been abandoned by God. From the looks of him you would never have guessed that he mattered to anyone, let alone God. And of course, we could never be more wrong.

God's word to you from this account is that you are never abandoned.

Write this on your heart today: God's word to you from this account is that you are never abandoned. God knows you are waiting: for a corner to turn, a door to open, a new day to break. And He has not forgotten you.

Always remember what He told His other children when they thought they were forgotten: "Can a mother forget the baby at her breast and have no compassion on the child she has borne? Though she may forget, I will not forget you! See, I have engraved you on the palms of my hands" (Isa. 49:15–16).

7

The Man Who Could Do No Wrong

✦ Genesis 41:41–52 ✦

*What good is it for someone to gain the whole world,
and yet lose or forfeit their very self?*

—LUKE 9:25

Know thyself.

—SOCRATES

HAVE YOU EVER noticed that when in trouble, we call out to God a lot more than when things are going well? Of course you have . . . you're a human being. Have you ever noticed how we tend to forget Him when things are going well and default to handling things on our own? Of course we do . . . we're human beings. So I guess it's just human nature, really. But it's a fallen human nature, isn't it?

Yet God is still faithful. That same kind of pattern repeats itself all through the Bible and all too frequently for us to this day. People in trouble. God delivers them. People prosper. People forget all about God.

In the Genesis account, when His people were in trouble, facing a famine, God anticipated their dilemma and He used the circumstances of Joseph's life to get them into Egypt, where they were sheltered from that famine. Then four centuries later, when God's people were in trouble, in slavery in Egypt, God responded and used the circumstances of Moses' life to get them out.

And what a getting out it was! If you have ever watched the animated kid's movie *The Prince of Egypt*, you get a remarkable and imaginative kid's eye view of that. Disney's DreamWorks took the exodus account of Israel being rescued by God from slavery in Egypt and made it come to life for kids.

My daughter Rachel and her girls, eight and eleven at the time, were watching it together one day. There's this compelling depiction of the parting of the Red Sea that just captured the girls in the deepest places of their imagination. At that very moment, Kyra, the eleven-year-old, lost in the sparkling wonder of it all and just thinking out loud, said, "I can't believe they could ever worship idols after that."

Well, they did. The whining about God began in earnest about one week later. Then it only took about another month, in Exodus 16, for them to start talking about wanting to go back to Egypt and slavery. And not too much longer after that, they were worshiping the golden calf while Moses was getting the tablets of stone written by the hand of God, the Ten Commandments. People in trouble; God delivers. People prosper; God is forgotten.

My daughter reflected on that experience with her girls in conversation and then wrote about it on her blog. She lamented how at times, she was such an Israelite. And I can only wonder if I'm any different.

For her, God shows up in power and faithfulness to rescue her, and then she forgets, she said. She gives in to doubt or to her own ingenuity. Ah, her father's daughter, I'm afraid. We default to human nature so effortlessly, so seamlessly programmed to do so, but again, it's still a fallen human nature, isn't it?

So with great resolve my daughter wrote out a prayer to remind her of who she really was and who God really is: "God forgive me for all those times I have forgotten Your power so quickly, and doubted You and looked for my own answers. Don't let me forget my own moments at the Red Sea's edge, when You have parted the water for my rescue."

"Don't let me forget." But we so often do, don't we? Because human nature is fallen, disfigured by sin, its defaults don't lead us toward God; they lead away. They tend to place God on the back burner of life. A place where we keep Him until we need Him. Or worse, until we forget Him altogether.

The Bible has plenty of stories of people God took from nowhere significant and brought to somewhere magnificent. Like Moses, from a felon hiding on the backside of the desert to the greatest leader perhaps the world has ever known. David, who went from shepherd boy to king of Israel. And we get to read the stories of how they handled their newfound status.

But is there a more dramatic story with this kind of script than the story of Joseph? Joseph got promoted from forgotten foreign prisoner to secretary of agriculture of the greatest kingdom on earth, all in the same day. God had a lot of loose threads, dangling promises out there that He made to Abraham, Isaac, and Jacob that needed tying up. He began to tie them up—all through Joseph. And suddenly, all those boyhood dreams he had didn't seem so far-fetched.

> The Bible has plenty of stories of people God took from nowhere significant and brought to somewhere magnificent.

It begged the obvious question: Would it all go to his head? Would he be like us and forget God? Put God on the back burner?

In the heady atmosphere of such a stunning rise to prominence, from impotence and obscurity to potent power and celebrity, would he forget the one who got him there? Genesis 41:41–52 holds that answer for us.

> So Pharaoh said to Joseph, "I hereby put you in charge of the whole land of Egypt." Then Pharaoh took his signet ring from his finger and put it on Joseph's finger. He dressed him in robes of fine linen and put a gold chain around his neck. He had him ride in a chariot as his second-in-command, and people shouted before him, "Make way!" Thus he put him in charge of the whole land of Egypt.
>
> Then Pharaoh said to Joseph, "I am Pharaoh, but without your word no one will lift hand or foot in all Egypt." Pharaoh gave Joseph the name Zaphenath-Paneah and gave him Asenath daughter of Potiphera, priest of On, to be his wife. And Joseph went throughout the land of Egypt.
>
> Joseph was thirty years old when he entered the service of Pharaoh king of Egypt. And Joseph went out from Pharaoh's presence and traveled throughout Egypt. During the seven years of abundance the land produced plentifully. Joseph collected all the food produced in those seven years of abundance in Egypt and stored it in the cities. In each city he put the food grown in the fields surrounding it. Joseph stored up huge quantities of grain, like the sand of the sea; it was so much that he stopped keeping records because it was beyond measure.
>
> Before the years of famine came, two sons were born to Joseph by Asenath daughter of Potiphera, priest of On. Joseph named his firstborn Manasseh and said, "It is because God has made me forget all my trouble and all my father's household." The second son he named Ephraim and said, "It is because God has made me fruitful in the land of my suffering." (Gen. 41:41–52)

Back in another lifetime, I was in the grocery business, floor-level management. And I think anyone in any business would say his is a cut-throat world. But in the grocery business it's just awful. It was cruel how people got treated. We used to say, "Get as far up the ladder as fast as you can and hold on for as long as you can, because the rung you are standing on today could be gone tomorrow."

It was during those days when I was rising in the company that I met a man who was descending. It was like two escalators in a shopping mall. I was going up. He was going down. And as we passed each other on the fickle corporate escalator, he gave me this piece of sage advice: "Never lose your taste for hot dogs."

What he was saying, of course, was that there will be days of steak and champagne at the top, but someone will take it all away from you someday. In a heartbeat. So never lose your taste for hot dogs. Never forget who you are and where you've come from.

And Joseph didn't. He never forgot that all he ever was, God made him to be. Joseph never lost track of his essential identity. Oh, Pharaoh tried to Egyptianize him. He gave him an Egyptian wife from a priestly family whose political power and influence in the land was unmatched. Politically it would be like marrying into the 1960s version of Camelot, the Kennedy family.

> Joseph knew what it meant to be favored and how it could never insulate him from calamity.

The Pharaoh also gave him an Egyptian name whose best translation is perhaps "The One Who Knows." How ego inflating is that? Pharaoh gave him power and authority second to only his own. In all the land only Pharaoh himself would not have to bow to him.

Then he got the limousine chariot treatment: an entourage to escort him everywhere. No one was empowered to do anything in all the land apart from his word. He had status, prestige, and prosperity . . . on top of which, as we learned back in Genesis 39, he was well-built and handsome. He was pure Hollywood. Joseph had it all!

But he never lost his taste for hot dogs. Joseph knew what it meant to be favored and how it could never insulate him from calamity. He was favored once before. Remember? Joseph had been his father's favorite. And he knew how quickly that could all be taken away—and how easily the escalator up could become the escalator down.

He had also already learned, in his disappointing experience with the cupbearer, that trusting in people did not bring the kind of results that came with trusting God. When the cupbearer forgot him when he most needed to be remembered, Joseph learned the often empty value of trusting men. And besides, a Pharaoh who cut off the head of his chief baker on a whim was not a man to whom you entrusted your future.

In Acts 7, in his eloquent defense at his trial, Stephen cited Joseph as a great example of trust in God. "But God was with [Joseph] and rescued him from all his troubles" (vv. 9–10).

The key for us to remember is that until the rescue and exaltation were complete, Joseph was trusting God in the midst of great hardship and struggle. Yet, in slavery, in prison, everywhere he went, the text repeatedly says that God was with him.

And to me, here is the intriguing thing the text is trying to tell us. Through his trust in God, Joseph brought the blessing of God into his pagan master's home and then again into the prison cell where he languished. Joseph became a blessing carrier.

> Joseph became a blessing carrier.

By trusting God, Joseph saw God's hand at work in even the darkest moments of his life. Could it be that God has you where He does right now so you can bring the blessing of God into that context?

Do you remember Dietrich Bonhoeffer? He was martyred in Nazi Germany. Writing from the death camp in which he died, he said, "I have discovered that having God is enough."[1] How could he say that? Bonhoeffer had learned something about the meaning of life. If your meaning in life comes from knowing God, then the thing that gives your life meaning can never be taken away.

And Joseph discovered that very thing. God was the source of meaning for his life. You could take away Joseph's coat of many colors, take away his father and family and home, take away his status as a free man, his creature comforts, and even throw him in prison, but no one could take away from him the thing that made life meaningful for him: his relationship with God.

> If your meaning in life comes from knowing God, then the thing that gives your life meaning can never be taken away.

You see, life can be rendered meaningless for us if the thing that makes life meaningful for us is removed or devalued or marginalized. If you live for status and your status is taken away, your life has just become meaningless. Do you fall apart when someone passes you by at work or at school? What does that say about your values and priorities?

If you find your meaning in life from your work or your wealth, from your hobbies or your interests, from your kids or your spouse or your looks, know this: all those things can be taken from you in life, or devalued or marginalized. Then what? You have lost your source of meaning in life.

But Joseph found out that God could not be taken away from him. God was with Joseph everywhere he went: favoring him, blessing him, keeping him . . . and shaping him. First there was the Joseph who might rub us the wrong way. He was the petulant teenage boy who seemed so naively full of himself. But the Joseph we love and admire was the one who became a man of God during thirteen years of slavery and prison. Look what it took to transform him. The thing you would think would break him, actually made him, because God was with him.

I remember a story, only vaguely now, from the collected work of Dostoyevsky, that casts light on what prison does to a person. One character in the story, who was imprisoned for years in a labor camp, was forced to work in a government factory. Over the years he collected up bits of wire and stuffed them into a bottle. When he got out, he broke the bottle.

While the bottle shattered into a hundred pieces, the wires he jammed into it all those years remained intact. They still carried the shape of the bottle. Dostoyevsky's point was clear: in effect, the man was freed from prison, but never freed from what prison made him into.

Joseph on the other hand, had spent thirteen years in slavery and prison, and what did he say when he got out? It was written in the names of his sons. "God has caused me to forget all my trouble . . . God has made me fruitful in the land of my suffering" (Gen. 41:51–52). Joseph was shaped by God in his imprisonment, and not by prison itself. And that only happened because he trusted God and found that that was meaning enough for life, even in hard places.

Pharaoh tried everything to Egyptianize Joseph, but he could not Egyptianize his soul. How do we know? Again, it was seen in what he named his sons. He did not give his sons Egyptian names. He gave his sons Hebrew names that reflected not only his continued trust in God, but the reality of who God was to him. God was the one who had healed his past, and God was the one who was responsible for the power and prosperity he now had.

> Joseph was shaped by God in his imprisonment and not by prison itself.

It was God who made him forget his troubles, not Pharaoh, with his shower of prestige and power. It was God who made Joseph fruitful, not Pharaoh and his gifts and

grandeur. Joseph knew who was responsible for his elevation in life. He knew who deserved the credit. In the midst
of his very human glory, when human nature was shouting,
"Make way for Joseph! Make way for Joseph!" Joseph wasn't
about to forget God. When he got to the top of the escalator,
he kept his head. As someone who has ridden the corporate
escalator, I wonder if I would have.

How easy it would have been to lose God in the midst
of all that personal prosperity. Fallen human nature being
what it is, you would expect that. But it does not have to be
that way. My daughter wrote about it in on her blog. Joseph
proved it with his sons' names.

Every time he called them in from play or called to them
across the lawn in front of his palace, he was calling out for
everyone to hear: "God has made me forget all my troubles
. . . God has made me fruitful in the land of my suffering."

Human nature tends to make God forgettable. But with
this choice Joseph was making God unforgettable. Ask yourself what choices you are making in your life that are making
God unforgettable.

It seems there are two things
to remember from this account:
one is who we are and the other
is who God is . . . and all He has
done for us. If you and I have
forgotten who we really are,

> With this choice
> Joseph was making
> God unforgettable.

fallen human nature will want to enthrone us, tell us that
we are only what we make of ourselves, that we need to look
out for number one.

But the starting point for our identity in the Bible is
totally different. The Bible doesn't want us to forget who we
really are and what God has done for us: "You were dead
because of your sins and because your sinful nature was not
yet cut away. Then God made you alive with Christ, for he
forgave all our sins" (Col. 2:13 NLT). Anything we are in God
at all is not our doing. It's His.

I see it like this: Imagine, if you can, a hospital for dead people. The dead arrive and, amazingly, they are nursed back to life. They get revived somehow; they get renewed strength every day, until eventually, once they are fully well, they are released from the hospital.

Well, imagine two patients—let's call them Bob and Tom. They are getting stronger every day . . . soon to be released, in fact. And today finds them sitting in the cafeteria, shooting the breeze, eating nice, greasy cheeseburgers. I mean, if you can get away with it, why not? While they are eating, one of the new patients, just brought back to life a day or two ago, is rolled up in a wheelchair to the table right beside them. The new guy orders only soup. It's all you can stomach if you've just recently been dead, right?

Bob leans over and whispers to Tom, "See that guy? When they brought him in, man, he was *really* dead! I mean dead! Now, me, I wasn't as bad as that. I was only *mostly* dead. I just needed some minor repair work done."

And Tom says, "Yeah, me too. I wasn't in that bad a shape. I'm here to tell ya, I didn't need all the work he needed. In fact, I was in such good shape, they said they were surprised I even showed up at the hospital door."

I run into Christians all the time who talk and behave like this. They act as though they didn't need as much rescuing as this person or that person. It is called self-righteousness. They act as if, though begun by the Spirit, they are now being perfected by the flesh, by their own efforts. They talk as if they are the product of their own manufacturing. They don't need God anymore, it seems. You know what? They've lost their taste for hot dogs.

And from my caring pastor's heart, I want to scream: "Are you nuts? You were dead! Completely and utterly spiritually dead! It took as much to bring you to life in Christ as it took anyone! And what it took was Christ. All you are ever going to be is who God forms you to be."

Paul told the church in Corinth:

Brothers and sisters, think of what you were when you were called. Not many of you were wise by human standards; not many were influential; not many were of noble birth. But God chose the foolish things of the world to shame the wise; God chose the weak things of the world to shame the strong. God chose the lowly things of this world and the despised things—and the things that are not—to nullify the things that are, so that no one may boast before him.

It is because of him that you are in Christ Jesus, who has become for us wisdom from God—that is, our righteousness, holiness and redemption. Therefore, as it is written: "Let him who boasts boast in the Lord" (1 Cor. 1:26–31).

When you forget God, you forget your spiritual roots. And when you forget God, you are, in fact, using Him. It's as if you got what you wanted, and now you don't need Him; you can handle life on your own.

Tell me: who ever likes to be forgotten? When you are forgotten, you feel as though you didn't matter. You feel used. You feel cheapened.

Well, imagine how God must feel when He liberates us from sin, saves us from our foibles and mistakes, rescues us in all of our Red Sea moments, and then we forget Him. It is why the book of Deuteronomy says repeatedly, "When you get into the land that flows with milk and honey, don't forget who got you there" (paraphrased).

Could it be that that is why Jesus committed His memory to the bread and the cup of the communion table? He didn't commit His memory to the cross or the empty tomb or to some church building. We are the ones who do that. He committed His memory to the bread of everyday life and the wine of the everyday table.

Why? He was simply saying, *Don't forget Me. Every time you sit down to eat and drink, remember Me. I am entrusting*

My memory to these common staples because I don't want you to forget Me in the commonness of life.

Remember what I have done for you. Remember how I have delivered you from sin and rescued you from sin's penalty. In other words, don't forget who you were, and don't forget who God is. Don't let it go to your head. Never lose your taste for hot dogs.

In the seven years of abundance, Joseph never forgot God. When the seven years of famine came, he was familiar with the sound of God's voice and the sense of God's presence.

> If we ignore Him in the seven years of plenty, we'll only find it harder to find Him in the seven years of famine.

Let us not forget Him in the abundant years. Let's not forget who we are and who He is and all He has done for us. Let's not lose our taste for hot dogs.

Because when times of famine come, as they surely will; when life imprisons us, as it surely will, we'll need to be familiar with His voice and recognize the sense of His presence still with us. If we ignore Him in the seven years of plenty, we'll only find it harder to find Him in the seven years of famine.

8

The Not-So-Glad Reunion

✦ Genesis 42:1–28 ✦

When the words of her elder son Esau were reported to Rebekah, she sent and called her younger son Jacob, and said to him, "Behold your brother Esau is consoling himself concerning you by planning to kill you."

—GENESIS 27:42 NASB

Eat and drink with your relatives; but do business with strangers.

—GREEK PROVERB

YESTERDAY. YESTERDAY YOU ran out of time to get that project finished. Yesterday you missed a chance to correct that problem you had with someone. Yesterday you forgot to pay that bill or return those shoes or make that call. And then there's the stuff for Goodwill, and the grocery list, and the grass, of course.

Yesterday. What a day. We've all been there. And when you head off to bed, you tell yourself you've never felt more ready to put a day to bed. You're so glad it's over with.

But something's not quite right. You have the kind of feeling you might have after a long, hot, sweaty summer day when you let your kids go to bed without a bath or you're too tired to make sure they brush their teeth. The feeling you have is incompleteness.

And you're right, of course. Yesterday is incomplete. The calls and the bills and the shoes and the grass and Goodwill all get carried forward into the next day. You awoke to them this morning like awaking to a sink full of dirty dishes. Truth be told, all of those loose threads from yesterday are waiting to be picked up all over again.

And in picking up those threads, you find some of them are heavier and longer than others . . . more like ropes and measured more in miles. And they are tied, not to the errands of yesterday or the busyness of yesterday. They are tied to the heartaches of yesterday: the bruises of life, the skirmishes in families, the words that wounded you, and the love that went unspoken. These are the scars of life that were yesterday.

> We discover that while we're *so* done with yesterday, yesterday is nowhere near done with us.

But these weightier, longer ropes reach further back than just yesterday. They are tied to countless yesterdays: some more painful than others but none without consequence. And we discover once more: while we're *so* done with yesterday, yesterday is nowhere near done with us.

In Genesis 42 there were ten men who could tell us exactly how that felt. They were the brothers of Joseph, and our text tells their story. Once upon a yesterday, they sold their brother into slavery, saying that *now* they would see what becomes of his dreams. *Well, their yesterday got carried forward into their today.* And in just the reading of it, we might readily find ourselves in their sandals: face-to-face with the consequences of a yesterday we thought we'd never hear from again.

When Jacob learned that there was grain in Egypt, he said to his sons, "Why do you just keep looking at each other?" He continued, "I have heard that there is grain in Egypt. Go down there and buy some for us, so that we may live and not die."

Then ten of Joseph's brothers went down to buy grain from Egypt. But Jacob did not send Benjamin, Joseph's brother, with the others, because he was afraid that harm might come to him. So Israel's sons were among those who went to buy grain, for there was famine in the land of Canaan also.

Now Joseph was the governor of the land, the person who sold grain to all its people. So when Joseph's brothers arrived, they bowed down to him with their faces to the ground. As soon as Joseph saw his brothers, he recognized them, but he pretended to be a stranger and spoke harshly to them. "Where do you come from?" he asked.

"From the land of Canaan," they replied, "to buy food."

Although Joseph recognized his brothers, they did not recognize him. Then he remembered his dreams about them and said to them, "You are spies! You have come to see where our land is unprotected."

"No, my lord," they answered. "Your servants have come to buy food. We are all the sons of one man. Your servants are honest men, not spies."

"No!" he said to them. "You have come to see where our land is unprotected."

But they replied, "Your servants were twelve brothers, the sons of one man, who lives in the land of Canaan. The youngest is now with our father, and one is no more."

Joseph said to them, "It is just as I told you: You are spies! And this is how you will be tested: As surely as Pharaoh lives, you will not leave this place unless your youngest brother comes here. Send one of your number to get your brother; the rest of you will be kept in prison, so that your words may be tested to see if you are telling the truth. If you are not, then as surely as Pharaoh lives, you are spies!" And he put them all in custody for three days.

On the third day, Joseph said to them, "Do this and you will live, for I fear God: If you are honest men, let one of your brothers stay here in prison, while the rest of you go and take grain back for your starving households. But you must bring your youngest brother to me, so that your words may be verified and that you may not die." This they proceeded to do.

They said to one another, "Surely we are being punished because of our brother. We saw how distressed he was when he pleaded with us for his life, but we would not listen; that's why this distress has come on us."

Reuben replied, "Didn't I tell you not to sin against the boy? But you wouldn't listen! Now we must give an accounting for his blood." They did not realize that Joseph could understand them, since he was using an interpreter.

He turned away from them and began to weep, but then came back and spoke to them again. He had Simeon taken from them and bound before their eyes.

Joseph gave orders to fill their bags with grain, to put each man's silver back in his sack, and to give them provisions for their journey. After this was done for them, they loaded their grain on their donkeys and left.

At the place where they stopped for the night one
of them opened his sack to get feed for his donkey,
and he saw his silver in the mouth of his sack. "My
silver has been returned," he said to his brothers.
"Here it is in my sack."
  Their hearts sank and they turned to each other
trembling and said, "What is this that God has done
to us?" (Gen. 42:1–28)

"Why do you just keep looking at each other?"

Levi shot a furtive glance at his brother Simeon. Reuben
eyed a guilty-looking Issachar up and down to make sure he
didn't crack. Asher, another brother, just stared at his feet,
while others pretended not to notice what was said.

The famine was threatening everything. Talk about loose
threads. Life for all of them was hanging by a badly frayed
thread. It was like a death grip getting tighter and tighter on
the whole tribe, and they were doing nothing . . . just staring
at each other. Why? Because the
elephant they thought was dead
had come back into the room.

It was an elephant named
Egypt. Nobody wanted to talk
about Egypt. Egypt was the only
place on the whole earth that had
grain. But Egypt was also the
place where Joseph was. It was
the place where they sold him into
slavery. They couldn't go down

> Joseph had twenty
> years' worth of
> very remarkable
> experience with
> God. His brothers?
> They were still
> stuck in who they'd
> always been.

there. They didn't have any idea that he was a ruler there
now, or that he was even alive. But what if?

A guilty conscience is always tied up in knots by the
what-ifs. It is why Solomon wrote, "He who walks in integrity
walks securely" (Prov. 10:9 NASB). The person with a clean
conscience can sleep at night and not worry about yesterday

coming back and biting him. But this bunch is nothing but sleepless.

For twenty years these brothers had buried their sin against Joseph in some deep corner of their conscience. But with the famine, Egypt brought it all back up on the radar screen. And the very mention of Egypt awakened a thousand guilty thoughts from a long-ago yesterday they thought they'd never have to deal with again. They were *so* done with that yesterday. But it was not done with them.

Over the past twenty years, Joseph had trusted God in hard circumstances, and God had transformed him into a great man. God had not just exalted him to become a ruler in Egypt, but as we have learned in this study of his life, God had healed Joseph's heart, taught him to trust, vindicated him time and again, preserved and protected him, and so on. Joseph had flourished in his open-hearted, face-to-face relationship with God. Joseph had twenty years' worth of very remarkable, very personal, and intimate experience with God.

And his brothers? They were still stuck in who they'd always been. They had not changed. All they had was twenty more years of mileage on the odometer of life. Twenty years later found them so crippled by guilt they couldn't even begin to think about going down to Egypt. They were watching their families suffer and their livestock die, but they were paralyzed by a guilty conscience. William Shakespeare wrote in the play *Hamlet*, "Conscience makes cowards of us all."[1] They could not look God in the face. They could not even look their father in the face.

The human conscience is a curious part of our nature. It's that God-given, built-in moral compass that is supposed to make us feel guilty for doing wrong. But as the last chapter underscored, our human conscience is as fallen as our human nature. It is distorted by original sin. We're behind before we even begin. It doesn't work right, and then we go and make the situation worse.

One writer compared the human conscience to a sundial. A sundial gives you a fairly accurate reading of time during the light of day but doesn't help a whole lot in the dark of night. And that is where we like to keep our conscience: in the dark. And don't we all know a thousand ways to keep it there? We cover it over with flawed reasoning and clever rationalizations. We bury it under repeated deceits. We lull it to sleep with droning apathy.

Finally, it seems, when we've postponed dealing with things long enough, we figure we've got it beat. It's as if we've trained our conscience like the family dog. Whistle once and it stands up. Whistle twice and it rolls over. Whistle three times and it plays dead.

We'd like a lot of our yesterdays to do just that, wouldn't we? Roll over and play dead and stay dead. Don't trouble us. Don't give us any grief. Just go away. We are so done with yesterday. But in our hearts, we know that yesterday is not done with us. It is still affecting us.

Earlier I shared a story from my childhood about being lost at a carnival and the angst that it caused . . . abandonment issues and so on. (And yes, I was found.) But it triggered another childhood story of a type of discipline that was used in our home: threats. When my parents got exasperated with me, they used to threaten to sell me to the gypsies, who apparently were always in the market for unwanted kids.

I might smile at it now, but as a five- or six-year-old kid back in the '50s, that was a real fear. Especially when the threat was made and then I would be thrown in the car, and my father would begin to drive me down the street. It was terrorizing. (And for the record, he didn't sell me to the gypsies!)

That is a yesterday I am done with, but I learned later in life that it was not done with me. As the saying goes, "It explains a lot"—about the defaults in my response to matters of relational security and how I understood the love of God as Father. To grow up and to mature as a Christian, I have had to work that through so God could cut the rope and free me from the ways it was holding life back for me.

God doesn't want us tied to our past in unhealthy ways. He wants to transform you and me into a Joseph, not leave us tied up in knots of guilt, as Joseph's brothers were. God loves us too much to leave us starving in Canaan because we cannot face the what-ifs. His plan is to untie the rope that runs back to a burdensome yesterday that we've been dragging around for years. He wants to set us free.

There is a sort of wrestling match going on: all the while we are trying to keep our conscience in the dark and lull it to sleep, God is trying to wake it up and shine the light of His truth on it. He knows that if we deal faithfully with our yesterdays, our todays and tomorrows will look more like what Joseph experienced in Egypt than what his brothers experienced in Canaan.

How did God go about all this for Joseph's brothers? Well, He forced them to face their past. And it took a famine to do it. It took a near-death experience, death by starvation, to get them to face their past sin. God forced them to go to the last place on earth they would have chosen to go: Egypt. As an aside, it makes me wonder, would it take a near-death experience for us to face our past?

> You can no more absolve yourself of your own guilt than you can sit in your own lap.

The brothers probably thought that over time the guilt of what they had done would eventually go away. But as we've figured out already in this study, you can no more absolve yourself of your own guilt than you can sit on your own lap. And that guilt keeps distorting how we act and behave and think.

You know that experience when someone in the family walks in the door at the end of the day and starts biting your head off for no reason? We've all been there. But then we find out that he or she had a terrible day, and you say to yourself, *Well, that explains it.* Guilt has that same sort of disabling effect: it makes us behave in ugly, destructive, deformative ways.

But God won't leave us in that kind of space any more than He left the brothers of Joseph there. He's in the business of awakening in us the things that are destroying us and disfiguring life for us so we can deal with them and find out what life was supposed to be like.

> God doesn't want us tied to our past in unhealthy ways.

He does that by awakening the sleeping giant of our conscience. At times, it takes drastic measures: like a famine. It's no coincidence or accident. The text says earlier that it was God who brought the famine upon the whole earth, and He did it for a reason—ten reasons called *Joseph's brothers.*

I wonder if God still does that. Does He bring a famine in our lives to force us back to Him . . . back to the only One who can help us deal with our stuff? Intuitively, I think we all know that He does. Because given what life is, we don't want to face our stuff. It can be painful and inconvenient and embarrassing and humbling. It's the yesterday we don't want to deal with. But He loves us too much to leave us back there.

And so the famine comes. A famine of peace or contentment. A famine of joy or fulfillment. You have had your way up till now. You've managed. You've gotten by. But as one translator put it in Psalm 106:15: "And he gave them their request; but sent leanness into their soul" (KJV). You got what you wanted but got leanness of soul along with it.

The prophet Amos wrote, "'The days are coming,' declares the Sovereign LORD, 'when I will send a famine through the land—not a famine of food or a thirst for water, but a famine of hearing the words of the LORD. People will stagger from sea to sea and wander from north to east, searching for the word of the LORD, but they will not find it'" (8:11–12).

There is a personal famine, an inner famine, an inner hunger in us that only God can fill. And David's descriptive word for it is *leanness*. It's a God-given leanness of soul. Could it be that God has brought a famine in your life and mine so that we will finally deal with a yesterday we thought we'd never have to deal with again?

God is knocking at the door of your conscience if the knock is sharp and precise. There is a kind of empty or vague, foggy guilt that Satan traffics in. He uses it to keep us defeated and discouraged long after God has forgiven us.

You know that kind of feeling. We don't know why we feel so unworthy and unforgiven when we keep hearing how God loves us and has forgiven us so completely. If you experience that kind of foggy guilt, know this: it is not from God.

But when God wants to set you free from a guilty conscience, he is completely unambiguous. It is like David-and-the-prophet-Nathan kind of stuff: "Thou art the man!" (See 2 Samuel 12:1–7.) So take notice, then, as the account unfolds, how God deals with the brothers with just such precision.

> Could it be that God has brought a famine into your life and mine so that we will finally deal with a yesterday we thought we'd never have to deal with again?

It begins with surprise. We are kind of taken aback by Joseph and his harsh words and treatment of his brothers. It doesn't seem like the Joseph we know. And we wouldn't blame him if his anger was genuine.

Joseph had a lot to resolve from his past, and it all turned around his brothers who betrayed him. Just think about your own family system and the countless smaller betrayals you've endured. If you were in Joseph's sandals, think of how you might feel with all the power to do what you please with family members who did what they pleased with you when they held all the power.

Anger, vengeance, getting even. All of them come to the surface of our hearts pretty easily.

But Joseph's anger was feigned, and God was very much in this harsh treatment. God was using Joseph to bring his brothers to a place of complete repentance. And the only way that could happen was for them to take total ownership of their sin. So completely out of character and in a complete pretense, Joseph walked his brothers through an old scene from their past, only now the roles were reversed.

The clue was way back in Genesis 37, where the text said that Joseph had brought a bad report about his brothers. From that point on, his brothers saw him as little tattletale who spied on them for their father. Later in that chapter, when Jacob sent Joseph to check on his brothers and bring them food, they assumed he had come not to serve their best welfare but to spy on them again. They treated him cruelly and exercised total arbitrary power over him. They treated him as though he were a spy.

Now the roles were reversed. Joseph feigned anger and told them they hadn't come for food, but in fact, he accused them of being spies. And we know it's all an act because he had to take a time-out to cry over finally seeing his family again. But with every callously spoken word, the brothers were brought face-to-face, detail by detail, with their sin against Joseph.

Notice Genesis 42:21. They were cruel and arbitrary in the exercise of their power over their little brother; now they recognized their own sinful treatment of Joseph in the way this Egyptian ruler treated them. And they unwittingly acknowledged it all, coming clean in Joseph's presence.

When God forces us to face our past, to deal with issues of conscience, it is the full light of His Word and the full scope of the truth that get turned on the sundial of our conscience. He wants us to see our past for what it is, to sense its impact so that our repentance from it will be full-hearted and not halfhearted. If we are ever going to move from living at the level of Joseph's brothers and moving on into the life of blessing we are meant to experience, we must deal with all of yesterday, not just a few scattered pieces of it.

Have we ever considered that the seemingly harsh places of life show us more of the providence of God than we acknowledge? Could it be that the gifts and blessings of God come wrapped in the fiercest of paper? There is more of God in hard places than we might realize.

And to understand what God is up to in times of famine, we need to be asking Him the right questions. Not "Why don't You get me outta this jam?" but rather, "What does this circumstance mean? What are You trying to show me in this?" Because it just might be that He's knocking on the door of your conscience because He has a higher plane He wants you to live on and a greater experience of freedom for you to discover.

And don't be surprised if God uses the experience of prison as part of the solution in dealing with your troubling yesterdays. Probably for the first time in their lives, the brothers were completely vulnerable to someone who wielded absolute power over them. And Joseph used that power in an arbitrary way as they once did over him, ignoring their pleas as they had ignored his, and they are thrown into prison with no idea if or when they would ever get out, much like Joseph under Potiphar.

> [T]he gifts and blessings of God come wrapped in the fiercest of paper.

They were finding out firsthand what the consequence of their sin was like for the one they hurt. There were twenty years of sin's calluses built up over their hearts. It would take more than a slap on the wrist to crack through them. God would have to use the experience of prison to break through.

And when you read verse 21, you see that He did. In the darkness of prison, the light of repentance came on. For the first time in this whole story, the brothers acknowledged their wrongdoing. But it took the isolation and solitude of prison to do it.

It seems that when God wanted to transform Joseph, He did it in prison. When He wanted to break these brothers out of twenty years of stubborn refusal to repent of their sin, He used prison. Could it be that when God wants to do some new work in us, some inner healing or deep work that is meant to set us free from our yesterdays, He puts us in a life circumstance that can feel like prison?

We are made to feel powerless. It is as if something arbitrary is happening to us that we cannot argue with or reason our way out of. We are made to feel isolated, as though we are in solitary confinement. All the usual supports in life get taken away, and it is just us with our conscience and God with His presence, and that's where the wrestling begins. And like Jacob at the river Jabbok, we might walk with a limp afterward, but we know we have met God and we are not the same people we used to be.

Friend, does God have you isolated these days? Has He brought you to a place in your walk with Him where He has your undistracted attention? A place of solitude that may even feel like a prison or a desert? Don't panic. Trust Him. And listen for His voice. Three days later, the brothers were called out of prison. He will call you out of yours when His work in you is done.

The work He wants to do in you may very well be about repentance. As with Joseph's brothers, there may be something in your past that you need to own. And what you will find is that repentance is seldom instant. It's more of a process. It takes time. Like you and your family. We find that repentance is seldom immediate and that years of denial can make reconciliation within any family an enormous longer-term task.

But that is not the only reason God takes people into the desert. Time with God in a desert or a prison can also be about how to understand some destructive yesterday when your father threw you in the car and started to drive down the street. Abuse. Shaming. Fear. Not all of the yesterdays that disfigure us were of our making. So don't misread time in the desert as punishment. Always remember to trust. God was with Joseph in all of his hard places.

> [W]hen God wants to do some new work in us, He puts us in a life circumstance that can feel like prison.

Through prison, through rehearsing their sins against Joseph, and through forcing them to face their past, in tough love God awakened the collective conscience of Joseph's ten brothers. It was not about shaming them. It was a kind of hard-edged grace of God that wanted these brothers to be set free, just as He wants to set us free.

But not all of God's grace has that kind of hard edge. Look at verses 28 and 35. God gave them their money back. They got grain to save their families, and they got it for free. They didn't deserve it, but they got it. It's called grace. And isn't it more than interesting that a heart out of tune with God can turn grace into something fearful, as both verses point out?

Romans 2:4 states that it is the kindness of God that leads to repentance. And by this act of soft, kind-hearted grace, for the first time since we began the story of Joseph, in verse 28 the brothers openly acknowledged the hand of God in their lives. This is a real triumph of grace. After twenty years of deceit and trying to cover up their sin, for the first time the brothers came to awareness that God was afoot in their lives.

But while they got it right, they got it wrong at the same time. When you have lived with a guilty conscience for so long, even good news feels bad. They totally misinterpreted the grace of God in Joseph giving them their money back. "What is this God has done to us?" they asked. They were frightened. They were afraid of the rest of the story coming out.

They had repented in some measure. There was more to follow, but at least they had acknowledged their sin and they were on the right track. But when they accepted God's hand at work in their lives, for the first time they realized that God must know their dark secret, their sin against Joseph, the thing they hid so well from their own father with an elaborate plan of deceit. They hid it all so well for so long, but God knew it all! *Yikes! Now He's really going to get us good!*

Solomon wrote, "The wicked flee though no one pursues" (Prov. 28:1). Joseph's brothers were still thinking like guilty people. God was trying to tell them they were on the right track, but they couldn't see it. God gave them grace, and they thought it was a trap. That it was some kind of setup. That He was really out to get them. That is how the guilty think, even after their guilt is removed. (Not that we would ever think that way!)

Could it be that the sidebar of Genesis 42 is for us to quit thinking like guilty people! God knows all your hidden secrets, the things you've tried to keep from everyone. He knows all about you and still loves you. In fact, He even likes you. God does not deal with us according to our sin but according to His matchless grace.

> When you have lived with a guilty conscience for so long, even good news feels bad.

And He knows it's not easy to deal with yesterdays. So all along the way, God sends us these little divine signals of His grace . . . like the unmerited favor of finding your money in your sack. Don't be afraid. It's not a trap. It's just His way of showing us that we are on the right track to untying ourselves from the bondage of yesterday.

9

Are You Sure You Want Alone Time with God?

✦ Genesis 42:29–43:14 ✦

So Jacob was left alone, and a man wrestled with him till daybreak.

—GENESIS 32:24

The difference between a moral man and a man of honor is that the latter regrets a discreditable act, even when it has worked and he has not been caught.[1]

—H. L. MENCKEN

THERE IS A *true* sinner's prayer and then there is the *real* sinner's prayer. The true sinner's prayer is, "God be merciful to me a sinner" (see Luke 18:13 KJV). The real sinner's prayer is, "God, if You get me out of this mess, I promise I'll be good." The first one is the right one, of course. But when we are most honest about it, the one we use most often is the second: "Lord, I'm in big trouble. And if You'll just get me out of it, I'll never do it again. I promise."

I think we've all prayed that prayer in one form or another over the years. You've got a kid you can't rein in; you've got an illness you cannot beat; you've got a relationship that goes irretrievably sideways; you've done something terribly wrong and you can't find your way out . . . time to pull out all the stops with the real sinner's prayer.

We all know it. When we find ourselves in a circumstance beyond our control, we cry out to God. We make promises about turning over a new leaf or doing something for God that we've long neglected to do. It's really not the sinner's prayer. It's the bargainer's prayer. We try to cut a deal with God. And it's always a deal we try to make exclusively on our terms.

But then, when the crisis has passed, when we've got things back under our control again, we go back to the old status quo way of living. The pressure lifts and life is manageable again. It's not perfect, but we're getting by. And the promises we've made get forgotten.

In Genesis 42, Joseph's brothers were caught in a situation beyond their control. Accused of being spies, thrown in prison, threatened with death, made to feel completely powerless. All of it, of course, could be traced back to their sin against their brother Joseph when they sold him into slavery.

> What we most often pray is really not the sinner's prayer. It's the bargainer's prayer.

But once they were free from it, what would they do? Once they were back in control of life, how would they live? Perhaps the question should be asked of us: How will you and I live once the immediate crisis is passed? There is a sinner's prayer and a bargainer's prayer. Which one will you rely on to resolve all the unprocessed stuff of life?

The text holds answers to such questions. Take a moment now and read it through and watch for God's answers.

When they came to their father Jacob in the land of Canaan, they told him all that had happened to them. They said, "The man who is lord over the land spoke harshly to us and treated us as though we were spying on the land. But we said to him, 'We are honest men; we are not spies. We were twelve brothers, sons of one father. One is no more, and the youngest is now with our father in Canaan.'

"Then the man who is lord over the land said to us, 'This is how I will know whether you are honest men: Leave one of your brothers here with me, and take food for your starving households and go. But bring your youngest brother to me so I will know that you are not spies but honest men. Then I will give your brother back to you, and you can trade in the land.'"

As they were emptying their sacks, there in each man's sack was his pouch of silver! When they and their father saw the money pouches, they were frightened. Their father Jacob said to them, "You have deprived me of my children. Joseph is no more and Simeon is no more, and now you want to take Benjamin. Everything is against me!"

Then Reuben said to his father, "You may put both of my sons to death if I do not bring him back to you. Entrust him to my care, and I will bring him back."

But Jacob said, "My son will not go down there with you; his brother is dead and he is the only one left. If harm comes to him on the journey you are taking, you will bring my gray head down to the grave in sorrow."

Now the famine was still severe in the land. So when they had eaten all the grain they had brought from Egypt, their father said to them, "Go back and buy us a little more food."

But Judah said to him, "The man warned us solemnly, 'You will not see my face again unless your brother is with you.' If you will send our brother along with us, we will go down and buy food for you.

But if you will not send him, we will not go down, because the man said to us, 'You will not see my face again unless your brother is with you.'"

Israel asked, "Why did you bring this trouble on me by telling the man you had another brother?"

They replied, "The man questioned us closely about ourselves and our family. 'Is your father still living?' he asked us. 'Do you have another brother?' We simply answered his questions. How were we to know he would say, 'Bring your brother down here'?"

Then Judah said to Israel his father, "Send the boy along with me and we will go at once, so that we and you and our children may live and not die. I myself will guarantee his safety; you can hold me personally responsible for him. If I do not bring him back to you and set him here before you, I will bear the blame before you all my life. As it is, if we had not delayed, we could have gone and returned twice."

Then their father Israel said to them, "If it must be, then do this: Put some of the best products of the land in your bags and take them down to the man as a gift—a little balm and a little honey, some spices and myrrh, some pistachio nuts and almonds. Take double the amount of silver with you, for you must return the silver that was put back into the mouths of your sacks. Perhaps it was a mistake. Take your brother also and go back to the man at once. And may God Almighty grant you mercy before the man so that he will let your other brother and Benjamin come back with you. As for me, if I am bereaved, I am bereaved." (Gen. 42:29–43:14)

I think most of us are willing to endure a lot of things in life so long as we can control the situation. The trouble comes when control over our life passes from our hands to somebody else's. When we lose the power to determine our own way, we turn in just about every direction to find answers.

But as James Boice once wrote: "We resist necessity."[2] And we don't like to submit to a will other than our own.

My wife is a case in point. On a Canadian winter Sunday morning in church, with a packed sanctuary, I was struggling with a terrible sore throat, losing my voice with every word I spoke as I went along. Then, out of the corner of my eye, I saw my Marilyn get up and leave the sanctuary. A few minutes later, she walked in, in front of everyone, came onto the platform, and presented me with a cup of hot tea with lemon.

While the whole church was saying, "Ahhh. Isn't that sweet?" I read aloud to the church the Post-it note that she had attached to the saucer: "Please don't mistake this for submission." After the laughter died down, I commented on how it takes real love to submit our will to another . . . to give up control to determine our own way takes both submission and self-giving love of the highest order.

That is why when we find ourselves in a circumstance beyond our control, usually in desperation we are extrinsically motivated to submit and acknowledge that it is God's world, not ours, and we must ultimately come to terms with Him.

> To give up control to determine our own way takes both submission and self-giving love of the highest order.

And that is what happened to Joseph's brothers in chapter 42. They were starved into going down to Egypt—the last place on the planet they wanted to go. They got a bucket of ice-cold water thrown onto their drowsy collective conscience as Joseph's harsh treatment of them awakened every detail of their harsh treatment of him. They were arbitrarily thrown into prison, rendered powerless, their pleas ignored . . . they lost control over their own lives, just as Joseph lost his because of them.

Then, when they were freed—all but Simeon, of course—and they found their silver in their grain sacks (that grace of God coming through Joseph, the grace of getting what they did not deserve), it triggered an awareness that God was afoot in their lives. And it frightened them because (as Genesis 42:28 says) they now knew that *God* knew their secret sin, their sin against Joseph, and there was no telling what God would do. *"What is this that God has done to us?"*

They found out what happens in a circumstance where they were not in control. They suddenly were made to acknowledge that it was God's world, not theirs. They were not in control anymore. They had to ultimately come to terms with Him.

There are a thousand ways God could have placed His people in Egypt. But He did it this way for the benefit of the brothers and, frankly, the whole family. This was the family God had chosen to make into a great nation. And yet this was the poster family for dysfunction. God needed to heal the family's brokenness before He could make anything great out of them.

Could that be why He is doing what He is doing in your family these days? He has plans to bless you, make more of your life together, but there is some groundwork that needs to be done. Have you thought of it in those terms?

God did His work among Jacob's sons in three stages. All three of the principals in the story (Joseph, his brothers, and Jacob) needed to be reshaped and grown forward in their walk with God. That is why we first read how God took Joseph down to Egypt and made him who he was: He grew him and matured him into a remarkable, godly man. And all of that happened for him in the powerless aloneness of slavery and prison.

In this part of the story, God had begun to work on the brothers who have lived in the brokenness of crippling guilt: unable, unwilling, and unschooled in how to get free from it. Their time alone in prison was a big step forward on the path to complete repentance and healing.

Then there was Jacob: the deceiver, the poor father, and the emotionally fractured man. What would become of him? There was a sense in which God had to turn the heat up high enough for Jacob to let go of control over his own life.

God gave him a new name in Genesis 35, the name Israel, which means "prince." Yet he didn't look much like a prince there, did he? Could it be that God intended to get him alone as He did with Joseph and then the brothers in order to reshape and rebuild him? Could it be that God intends to get *you* alone, to reshape and rebuild you? Well, with Jacob, we pick up the first clues when the brothers got home.

The immediate danger had passed; they were back in Canaan, with grain to live on; and circumstances were back under their control, and how did the boys behave? Did they act as if God was up to something in their lives? There was no mention of God at all in their accounting of the events to Jacob. Did they evidence any contrition or repentance for selling Joseph into slavery? "Joseph? Joseph who?"

Was there any inclination to come clean with their father about the sin that put the whole family at risk in the first place? Nope. It was right back to sin management. Spin control. Family status quo as usual. Back to a normal that was really abnormal.

A life of covered-over or disguised sin is not the same as a life of forgiven sin. Though the brothers thought that how they handled things was tolerable, God did not. He had a whole family to restore and repair, and it was not going to heal until everyone came clean.

The God who brought the famine in the first place, turned up the pressure as the famine became more severe. Again, He used extrinsic motivation to get the work done inside the heart of this family. He brought everyone face-to-face with

Egypt again: Egypt and Joseph. Egypt and the past nobody wanted to talk about honestly.

Jacob didn't handle it well. He began with a complaint full of self-pity. Notice verse 36. "Everything is against me!" He interpreted every hardship in life as the hand of God against him. Jacob sounds like my grandkids when they don't get their way. "Everybody is out to get me. No one will play with me." Many of you in this season of life know the drill.

It's as if you take the song "Jesus Loves Me" and change the words to suit your disposition:

No one loves me; this I know
My misfortune tells me so
So I sing this simple song
Everything just turns out wrong
Nobody loves me
Nobody loves me
Nobody loves me
My bad luck tells me so

That's how we see life when we cannot see past our own self-pity and find God's sovereign love and providence. *Everything is against me. Nothing has ever gone right for me.* When we are in that state, like Jacob, we so often fail to see what God is up to. God was not just trying to save Jacob and his family from the famine: He was trying to save them from themselves.

But in his self-pity, Jacob had forgotten the promises God made to him about making him into a great nation. Which, of course, only makes me wonder what promises God has given us that we may have forgotten in the midst of a current season of famine.

In his self-pity, Jacob simply and stubbornly refused to let Benjamin go down to Egypt in order to get Simeon back. Again, notice verse 38: Jacob refused to submit to a will other than his own because to do so was to lose the power to determine his own way. Because he could not see God's hand anywhere in the situation, he refused to let control over his life pass into the hands of somebody else. He was just stubborn and unsubmissive. Someone needed to bring him a cup of hot tea and lemon!

As I get older, I am learning to surrender in new ways. And the most humbling way is to my adult children. They still need me to be strong. They still need to rely on me. They still come to me for counsel. And they still like to think that I have three middle initials: ATM!

But in hundreds of small ways, there is a shift going on where I must step back or they will never be able to step forward. It's in simple things now, like sorting out computer stuff or technology . . . or advice on understanding culture shifts or important trends in generational thought. But I know there are bigger, more personal ways yet to come.

> I need to surrender control of some matters of family life or my children will never learn how to take up the mantle of leadership in our wider family life.

More and more, I need to give them the lead that I once took. I need to create that space for them to lead. I need to surrender control of some matters of family life or they will never learn how to take up the mantle of leadership in our wider family life. And that need to surrender will only increase. It's normal and natural. But, let's face it: it's pretty humbling to submit to your own kid.

In Jacob's story, there was a shift occurring: Jacob was losing power in the family. And Joseph was gaining it. The old dreams of Joseph were actually coming true. Jacob was going down the escalator and Joseph was going up. And the leadership gap between the two grew greater with every verse in this story.

In his stubbornness and self-pity, Jacob could not see the hand of God bringing any of His promises to pass. All he could see was himself, and that was not a very pretty sight, truth be told. How much better it is to move with God and find the joy of dreams fulfilled, than to sit wrapped in a cloak of self-pity while a future gets imposed upon you in painful ways. But he couldn't see it. None of it.

Isn't it interesting how we imagine that things will change if we ignore them? Look at Genesis 43:2. Jacob was in denial, and as we say in our household, "de-nile is not just a river in Egypt." Denying reality will not make reality change. A car in your driveway that won't start today is not going to start tomorrow if you just leave it for a day. Denial fixes nothing.

He tried whining in verse 6: "Why did you bring this trouble on me by telling the man you had another brother?" When life doesn't go our way, when our will is not the will that rules in life, we look for someone to blame, don't we? We are a culture of victims in America. In this case, the victim was Jacob. He would fit right in to twenty-first-century Western culture. Curiously, it was the brothers who, in true innocence for once, had no idea what telling Joseph about Benjamin would mean for Jacob and the family.

Finally, with death for his whole family staring him in the face, Jacob submitted to a will other than his own in verses 11–14. A grudging submission if ever there was one. Much like hot tea in the middle of a sermon.

But even then Jacob tried to influence the outcome with the exercise of his will by gathering gifts and luxuries of the day to present to the Egyptian ruler. Even to the end, he was trying to pull strings, trying to curry favor.

But notice verse 14: "May God Almighty grant you mercy before the man so that he will let your other brother and Benjamin come back with you." Here was where the worm turned. For the first time, Jacob openly acknowledged that it was into

> Isn't it interesting how we imagine that things will change if we ignore them? Denial fixes nothing.

God's hand that he was surrendering his will. His life and his future were not in the hand of some unknown Egyptian ruler. They were back where they always belonged, in fact, where they had always been: in God's hand. Only now, Jacob wouldn't be in the way, messing things up. Jacob gave up the fight of self-will and surrendered control over the future to where it always belonged: the hand of God.

But if he knew it was God all along, why did he fight so hard to hold on to Benjamin? Why did he resist what God was doing? Two important reasons suggest themselves.

The first was on a very natural level. Benjamin's mother was Rachel, Jacob's true love. Jacob worked seven years for his future father-in-law, Laban, to get Rachel, and was hoodwinked and given Leah instead, a wife the text says earlier that he never loved. He then worked seven more years to earn the right to have Rachel. And she gave him two sons: Joseph and Benjamin. Rachel, in Genesis 29, was described as lovely in form and beautiful. Joseph? He was well-built and handsome. He was his mother's son.

Rachel died giving birth to Benjamin, and understandably, Jacob was heartbroken and shattered by the experience.

> Jacob gave up the fight of self-will and surrendered control over the future to where it always belonged: the hand of God.

For the rest of his life he would look at Benjamin and see Rachel. Did Benjamin have his mother's eyes, the shape of her mouth, the color of her hair? We don't know. But we do know that his life was bound up in the life of that boy.

With Joseph gone, that made Benjamin not only the darling of Jacob's heart, but if he were to die, it would take the last living link to Rachel out of his life forever: a grief Jacob could not bear to even think about. That's just natural. We can understand that.

But there was a supernatural piece to this as well. Because he loved Rachel and not Leah, Jacob just assumed that the promises God made to him about making him into a great nation could only come through the wife *he* loved, the one *he* chose, Rachel, his beloved. God wouldn't choose one of the lesser sons to make the great nation from. It had to be a son from the wife he chose. It is why Genesis 42:38 reads the way it does: "My son will not go down there with you; his brother is dead and he is the only one left. If harm comes to him on the journey you are taking, you will bring my gray head down to the grave in sorrow."

In Jacob's thinking, with Joseph gone, Benjamin was the last link to the covenant God had made with him. If he disappeared as Joseph did, it would mean the covenant was dead and that God had rejected Jacob. Benjamin had to be protected at all costs or Jacob's life would end in failure. Imagine how paralyzing that thought would be to Jacob.

But God, in His severe mercy, had painted Jacob into a corner and forced him to release his grasp on Benjamin. Much like Abraham had his Isaac, Jacob had his Benjamin. And God needed to show Jacob that the covenant was not dependent upon the life of either Benjamin or Joseph. It rested with God. In fact, the Messiah, through whom all the nations of the earth shall be blessed, came from the tribe of Judah, a middle child born to an unloved wife.

Jacob fought with God to hold on to Benjamin for a very natural reason, but also for a supernatural one. There was a second compelling reason he resisted God's leading in this account. I think he was beginning to sense that God wanted to get him alone. And every time Jacob was alone with God, God triumphed and Jacob submitted. Only as Jacob read it: God always wins, I always lose. The clue is in Genesis 43:14.

For the first time in his recorded life, Jacob called God *El Shaddai* (God Almighty). When you read through the covenants God made with Abraham and Isaac and then Jacob, you find that El Shaddai was God's original deal-making name. He used it as a divine signal that something was important. And how much more important could it have been, the first time he used it in Genesis 17? It was spoken from God's own lips to Abraham as He made a covenant with him that still affects us to this day.

In Genesis 28, we heard it from the lips of Jacob's own father when the covenant was passed from Isaac to Jacob. Isaac sent Jacob off alone to find a wife, and on that journey, alone in the night, he saw a vision of a ladder ascending up to heaven. He heard the voice of God Almighty speaking to him in that vision, and God repeated His covenant promises to him. And Jacob surrendered there, building an altar to worship God, and in surrender to God, promised a lifetime of faithfulness to him.

Then, in chapter 35, God told Jacob to move away from his extended family, and there, out on his own, alone with God again, he was given another vision that rehearsed the covenant God had with him, and Jacob surrendered anew, worshiped God, and surrendered to His will.

There was a pattern there. God got Jacob alone; God renewed His covenant; Jacob surrendered his will to God and worshiped Him.

But the Old Testament experts who read this are thinking I've missed one: Jacob and God alone, wrestling at the river Jabbok the night before he was to meet Esau, the brother he'd cheated years ago, the brother the Bible says comforted himself with thoughts of killing Jacob. And much like the timing of Jacob's sons and Joseph, all of that was twenty years ago. Esau had time to think about how he'd like to do it. And Jacob, alone with God, had a lot to wrestle with that night. Would God keep the covenant alive by keeping Jacob alive, or would Esau end it all with one chop of a sword?

> God got Jacob alone; God renewed His covenant; Jacob surrendered his will to God and worshiped Him.

It was a night to remember. Jacob wrestled with the angel of God all night, and just when it seemed he might win, the angel touched his hip, displacing it, and Jacob walked with a limp for the rest of his days.

But I like how the prophet Hosea described the lifelong struggle of Jacob with God: "In the womb he grasped his brother's heel; as a man he struggled with God. He struggled with the angel . . . he wept and begged for his favor" (Hosea 12:3–4). There at the riverside in the morning, the angel of the Lord blessed Jacob and renewed the covenant one more time. Jacob showed his worshiping heart as he named the place of his encounter with God in honor of God.

Back in our text, God was using circumstances to wrestle Jacob into submission again. I think that Jacob was sensing that God was getting him alone once more, and he was resisting because he knew that to be alone with God was a wrestling match he could not win.

He knew it meant acknowledging who he really was and who he was not. And who he was, was not a towering spiritual giant of a man. He was an old, broken, sinful man with a lifetime of regrets and sorrows. Who he was not was what he had promised God he would be back in Genesis 28: faithful.

He knew what we know: that to be alone with God means that God will want to deal with all the issues none of us want to deal with. For Jacob that would look like releasing his grasp on Benjamin, the one he had been relying upon to be the guarantor of the promises of God for the tribe. Now his grasp would have to be on God and God alone.

For us that means surrendering all the areas of life we don't want to surrender. It will mean submitting to a will that is not our own, coming to terms with God on His terms, not ours. No bargainer's prayer. Just the true sinner's prayer.

But when God gets us alone and does the work He wants to do in us, a remarkable thing happens: we begin to experience the promises He has made to us. Peace, joy, and contentment. Hope, confidence, and assurance. His presence, power, protective love, and guidance. The promises of God's New Testament covenant are realized in new ways in our life. In sophisticated theological language of the erudite scholars, this Christianity stuff really begins to work.

Although he could not see it through his tears of regret and self-pity, when Jacob released Benjamin, he stepped right into the blessing of God. In the chapters that follow, he not only would get Benjamin back; he would get Simeon back, as well as Joseph.

Then in the years that followed, he saw all the family's broken relationships healed, he got to live in prosperity in Egypt to the ripe old age of 130 (putting all kinds of pressure on the Egyptian social security system!), and actually got to see his dysfunctional family become a great nation that he could not number. Not a bad exchange for surrendering your will to God, I'd say. God always uses aloneness with Him constructively and productively.

If you pray the bargainer's prayer, you never get the blessing that only comes with complete surrender. But even reluctant surrender is met with the blessing of God. So maybe all that is left for us is to answer the questions this account whispers.

Questions such as, Where are the circumstances of life taking you? Pressing you? Where do they pinch you? Can you find God's fingerprints there? I commonly tell young pastors that two things change the future: pain or vision. It takes pain to change the future for Jacob. What will it take for you and me?

> [E]ven reluctant surrender is met with the blessing of God.

As God the promise keeper pulls you toward Him, what is the promise you have never really kept, never really lived up to? You'll find that it's likely that thing you keep struggling with . . . the one you offered Him in a bargainer's prayer long ago. A bargain, it turns out, that you and I have never found the strength to really keep. As we discovered with Jacob's bargainer's prayer in Genesis 28, faithfulness is hard to maintain in your own strength.

Why does it seem that God is always wrestling with me? As Acts 26:14 says, "It is hard . . . to kick against the goads," isn't it? What is my Benjamin, the darling object of my heart that has become a sort of false sense of security or hope for me? Is it a job, a spouse, a child, a friend? Is it skill, a gift, my looks or my age or my money? How tight is the grasp?

And finally this: When was the last time God had you or me alone? Answer that and we could find an answer that explains a lot of what we are experiencing these days: be it a famine in our Canaan or the prosperity of Egypt we were meant to know and experience.

10

The Message Hanging
over Your Life
✦ Genesis 43:15–34 ✦

*Wretched man that I am! Who will set me free from the
body of this death?*

—ROMANS 7:24 NASB

*If you really want to hear about it, the first thing you'll
probably want to know is where I was born, and what
my lousy childhood was like, and how my parents were
occupied and all before they had me, and all that David
Copperfield kind of crap, but I don't feel like going into
it, if you want to know the truth.*

—J. D. SALINGER, *CATCHER IN THE RYE*

WORDS LINGER. THEY hang around. They leave their
mark. They turn the human memory into a tyrant who won't
let you forget the signs that got hung over your life early on.

So I'm talking with a thirty-something woman heading
into ministry with her husband: competent, bright, spiritually mature, outgoing, and full of giftedness. And also quite
broken. Left broken by a word that still lingers. It just won't
leave and let her be.

She was a fraternal twin with a sister who in every respect, it seemed, was the cuter, the more adorable of the two. Every time grandma came for a visit, her mom would dress them up for the occasion. Grandma would come through that door and immediately latch onto her sister. She would fawn over her, gush over her, telling her how her outfit just made her sparkle, and her shorts made her look like such a grown-up girl.

Then, as if in an afterthought, she would turn to her sister and say, "And yours are blue."

I could see it written on her face before her mouth even framed the words to complete the story for me. She felt diminished. Less than. Never enough. Never adequate. Never acceptable. So much less than worthy of love.

Solomon was right, of course: "Death and life are in the power of the tongue" (Prov. 18:21 NASB). You can speak messages of life that empower children to succeed in life beyond every expectation. And you can speak messages of death that kill dreams and blunt hopes and rob them of a thousand possibilities.

The apostle James wrote, "The tongue . . . is a restless evil, full of deadly poison. With the tongue we praise our Lord and Father, and with it we curse human beings, who have been made in God's likeness. Out of the same mouth come praise and cursing. My brothers and sisters, this should not be" (James 3:8–10). And is that ever true.

You can begin to imagine how all the messages of favoritism, spoken and unspoken, implied and practiced by Jacob for his two favored sons, affected the household of Jacob. Only two of the twelve boys really mattered to him: the sons he had with Rachel, his beloved. Joseph and Benjamin. Every other son was a tax deduction, and that was about it. They were less than. Never enough. Never adequate. Never acceptable. So much less than worthy of love. *And yours are blue.*

In his paternal blindness Jacob didn't even try to hide it. How could he when he gave the one son a nobleman's cloak of many colors, and when he disappeared, Jacob bound his heart so deeply to Joseph's younger brother that the other ten sons became invisible? In his relationship with his sons, he fawned over Joseph, cooed over Benjamin, and everyone else's were blue.

Jacob had hung a sign over his other sons' lives: a message of inadequacy and diminished worth. That was why Simeon was left wallowing in a prison in Egypt for two years. In the story line it seemed as though his loss was affordable, tolerable. Simeon in prison alone was not enough to motivate his father Jacob to send for his rescue. It would take his whole clan nearly starving to death before he was willing to put Benjamin at risk. Take a moment and refresh your heart with the story by reading the text:

> So the men took the gifts and double the amount of silver, and Benjamin also. They hurried down to Egypt and presented themselves to Joseph. When Joseph saw Benjamin with them, he said to the steward of his house, "Take these men to my house, slaughter an animal and prepare a meal; they are to eat with me at noon."
>
> The man did as Joseph told him and took the men to Joseph's house. Now the men were frightened when they were taken to his house. They thought, "We were brought here because of the silver that was put back into our sacks the first time. He wants to attack us and overpower us and seize us as slaves and take our donkeys."
>
> So they went up to Joseph's steward and spoke to him at the entrance to the house. "We beg your pardon, our lord," they said, "we came down here the first time to buy food. But at the place where we stopped for the night we opened our sacks and each of us found his silver—the exact weight—in the mouth of his sack. So we have brought it back with

us. We have also brought additional silver with us to buy food. We don't know who put our silver in our sacks."

"It's all right," he said. "Don't be afraid. Your God, the God of your father, has given you treasure in your sacks; I received your silver." Then he brought Simeon out to them.

The steward took the men into Joseph's house, gave them water to wash their feet and provided fodder for their donkeys. They prepared their gifts for Joseph's arrival at noon, because they had heard that they were to eat there.

When Joseph came home, they presented to him the gifts they had brought into the house, and they bowed down before him to the ground. He asked them how they were, and then he said, "How is your aged father you told me about? Is he still living?"

They replied, "Your servant our father is still alive and well." And they bowed down, prostrating themselves before him.

As he looked about and saw his brother Benjamin, his own mother's son, he asked, "Is this your youngest brother, the one you told me about?" And he said, "God be gracious to you, my son." Deeply moved at the sight of his brother, Joseph hurried out and looked for a place to weep. He went into his private room and wept there.

After he had washed his face, he came out and, controlling himself, said, "Serve the food."

They served him by himself, the brothers by themselves, and the Egyptians who ate with him by themselves, because Egyptians could not eat with Hebrews, for that is detestable to Egyptians. The men had been seated before him in the order of their ages, from the firstborn to the youngest; and they looked at each other in astonishment. When portions were served to them from Joseph's table, Benjamin's portion was five times as much as anyone else's. So they feasted and drank freely with him. (Gen. 43:15–34)

It was that famous theologian (not!), college basketball coach Rick Pitino, who once said, "If you tell the truth about your mistakes, they become part of your past. If you try to hide the truth, they become a part of your future."[1] When his own moral failures came to light, he at least took his own advice and "fessed up" as we say in the South. So although he was not the model of moral restraint, he made the right point: sins forsaken and forgiven, you leave behind. Sins you try to cover up, just keep springing up. Joseph's family was a case in point.

> "If you tell the truth about your mistakes, they become part of your past. If you try to hide the truth, they become a part of your future."
> —Rick Pitino

The boys were going back to Egypt because they were hungry. And going back there meant facing that apparent tyrant of a ruler who threw their brother Simeon in prison. It also meant, one more time, that they had to face their sin of selling their brother into slavery and all of its consequences. Their past just wouldn't go away.

While Jacob hung a message of inadequacy over the lives of ten of his sons, with their own flawed choices, the brothers hung a message over their own lives: of fear, shame, guilt, and tension. A father who crippled them ended up with sons who made crippled choices. Thus, the brothers were left in a double bind.

Now, do notice that going back to Egypt had nothing, or at best, very little to do with Simeon. Jacob's concern was for Benjamin, not Simeon. Simeon's plight was not even mentioned. He was not even part of the equation in reaching the decision to go back. The ten brothers were only going back because their households were starving.

I wonder how the brothers felt about Jacob's sliding scale of affection for them, and his habit of comparative assessment on the relative value of his sons. How did they feel knowing that he played favorites?

Ever feel that your parents liked one of your siblings more than you? Of course you did. You're human. In some cases it was completely true. Some kids you have parental chemistry with, and other kids seem harder to love. Yet in most cases, favoritism is mostly just a perception. But in the saga of Jacob and his sons, it was not even a question. Jacob openly loved Joseph and Benjamin more than the others.

> A father who crippled them ended up with sons who made crippled choices.

Because Simeon was only one of the ten, in the first half of Genesis 43, Jacob showed no inclination to go back to Egypt to get him. In 42:36, he lamented that Simeon was no more, but truth be told, he knew where he was and what he had to do to get him back. He just wouldn't do it. It was Judah, Simeon's full brother, who was pushing the agenda to go back. He had a brother in prison. He wanted him out.

And how far would Judah go to get him out? He put himself on the line to guarantee the safety of the favored little brother whom Jacob loved most—the darling of his father's heart, Benjamin. That was a big shift for Judah. He was the one back in chapter 37 who talked his brothers into selling the other favorite, Joseph, into slavery.

The message conveyed by Jacob's affections must have left the brothers feeling that they were pretty much disposable parts, and only Joseph and Benjamin truly mattered. Those two were the sainted sons.

How did they feel at the end of chapter 43, when Benjamin was favored at the feast with a portion five times greater than theirs? Were they as bothered by that as they once would have been? Can a leopard change its spots?

I've got a secret. And so do you. We all have our secrets. But some of them are dark. And it's those dark secrets that have the power to deform and disfigure life for us. We see it in Joseph's brothers, how twenty-two years of guilt had crippled them with fear and anxiety. They had this dark secret they hoped would never come to light. And it affected every choice they made.

On their last visit to Egypt, it came to the surface before Joseph, of all people. The brothers were in his presence, speaking in Hebrew, assuming this ruler of Egypt would not know what they were saying. And in front of him, they acknowledged their guilt to each other over their treatment of Joseph.

It was, in effect, a start down the road to repentance for them. But once they got back to Canaan safe and sound, it was back to the old status quo of living with their dark secret. They'd had a brush with God . . . but it hadn't moved them deeply enough to turn completely.

The thing about dark secrets is that they affect the posture of your soul. They become a self-imposed glass ceiling on our personal, spiritual, psychological, and moral growth. We see that clearly with Joseph's brothers. Simeon was in prison in Egypt, and the other brothers were back home in Canaan, but they were still imprisoned: by a fear and anxiety they had cultivated in the keeping of their sinful secret.

As much as we see it in them, we know it ourselves from hard personal experience. The psalmist David said in Psalm 32:3–5: "When I kept silent, my bones wasted away through my groaning all day long. For day and night your hand was heavy on me; my strength was sapped as in the heat of summer. Then I acknowledged my sin to you and did not cover up my iniquity. I said, 'I will confess my transgressions to the LORD'—and you forgave the guilt of my sin." That's why he said in the first two verses of the psalm:

"Blessed is the one whose transgressions are forgiven, whose sins are covered. Blessed is the one whose sin the LORD does not count against them and in whose spirit is no deceit."

Which pretty much begs the question: Which part of Psalm 32 are you living in? The heaviness of dark secrets kept and covered up, or the lightness and blessing of experiencing sins forgiven? That's the kind of question we can only answer for ourselves, isn't it? And from this text I only hold up the mirror of God's Word so we can see that question clearly.

As much as we all have secrets, I have no interest in knowing yours. But God does. Because He sees what it is doing to you. The insecurity and fear. The shame and inferiority. The gnawing guilt that consumes you and the way it stoops your heart and clutters up your soul with the trash of life.

Beloved, this was never the way we were meant to live. Joseph's brothers either. And of all the ways God could have gotten His people into the safety and shelter of Egypt, He chose a way that would ultimately set the ten brothers free from the bondage of their guilt. And He chooses that way for you and me as well. But it's a work in progress.

Over the years I have come to see repentance that way. Less of an instant response. More of a continual process that results in lasting change. Repentance is this whole idea of turning around and going the other way. It is acknowledging in godly sorrow that I was going the wrong way and then demonstrating the honesty of that acknowledgment by going the right way.

Well, the brothers had done the first part in some measure, but they hadn't started walking the right way yet. There was more repentance work that needed to be done.

Take a nut and a bolt and a wrench, for example. One way to imagine the task of repentance is to see it as trying to get a nut loose that has been rusted onto an old lawn mower. Some nuts turn easier than others. Well, these ten nuts known as Jacob's sons had twenty-two years of built-up rust all over them. They were going to need some penetrating oil and a whole lot of muscle to get them completely turned around.

And that was what Joseph was doing there. He was not dragging out some slow, emotionally tortuous revenge on his brothers. Like God, he was not in the business of getting even. Joseph was drawing out of them genuine, full, and complete repentance.

The first time they went down to Egypt, they were intentionally treated harshly by Joseph. That was step one. It was designed to awaken their sleepy and dulled conscience. So everywhere they turned during their days in Egypt, they heard the echoes of their own harsh treatment of Joseph. And once that conscience was awakened, their fear and anxiety only sharpened.

But this time, everything was different. They headed down to Egypt again, unsure and suspicious of the ruler whom they had to deal with. They were going into the encounter expecting the same harsh treatment, having not learned anything from the grace of having their silver returned from the first trip. (I pause and wonder if we learn from the kindness of God's grace to us.)

> A guilty conscience is always suspicious of grace, it seems.

When they got an invitation to his home and extravagant hospitality instead of harsh words and hostility, they thought it was a trap. A guilty conscience is always suspicious of grace, it seems. But you know that. You've seen it in the responses you are prone to get when you offer a kindness to someone trapped in guilt. He can't understand it. She can't interpret it accurately.

The invitation by Joseph was something usually reserved only for foreign dignitaries. But the gesture itself was only the first of six expressions of kindness by Joseph toward his brothers.

There was the lunch itself. It was not a soup-and-sandwich affair. It was an eye-popping, sumptuous feast, made only more opulent by the fact that they were all living in a time of severe famine. Then there was the reassurance of Joseph's steward about their money. Then Joseph kept his word and gave them their brother Simeon back safe and sound. They were given the social courtesy reserved for honored guests: water to wash their feet and feed for their donkeys. And when Joseph spoke with them, he spoke only blessing: his every word was kind and his every question showed genuine interest in their welfare.

Remind me again of what they had done to deserve such favored treatment? Right. Nothing. In fact, given their track record, what they deserved was actually the opposite. But as you might recall from Psalm 103:10, "[God] does not treat us as our sins deserve or repay us according to our iniquities" because, as that text says earlier, in verse 8 "the LORD is compassionate and gracious, slow to anger, abounding in love."

I need to point out that, for them, all of this kindness was being shown from a total stranger. They received all of Joseph's kindness while having no idea who he really was. They would head home after this thinking, *I guess living the status quo life is all right after all. We've fooled the moral universe one more time. Let's just go home and rebury the past all over again.*

God is pouring out kindness upon kindness on [those who don't know Jesus] (common grace the theologians call it), and they have no idea who the Source of it all is.

Which makes me think of those in our world who really don't know Jesus. They stand in the place of Joseph's brothers. God is pouring out kindness upon kindness on them (common grace, the theologians call it), and they have no idea who the Source of it all is.

Well, let me tell you who it is: it is the living God. And He is doing it not so you can go on back to your own Canaan and the crippled status quo of a fear-based life. He is doing it so you might be free from that life. You might think the status-quo life, crippled by guilt, is never going to catch up with you. But it does. Read the paper; watch the news; look at the harvest of pain such a life brings.

God is trying to spare you that. He is pouring out His love and grace and kindness on you so you might understand that there is a God who loves you. And that He gave His Son for you, that you might know freedom from guilt and shame and sin's crippling dominion over your life. You don't have to live that way. His Son is the truth and the life, and He is also the way out of the life you find yourself in.

The brothers came expecting, as it were, the wrath of God and were given the grace of God. As I wrote in the previous chapter, it is the kindness of God that leads to repentance (Romans 2:4).

And finally, all that kindness melted away the brothers' suspicion and fear. They let their guard down. They could relax. And the text tells us they did. "So they feasted and drank freely with [Joseph]" (Gen. 43:34).

Freely. I love that word. They were freer than they had ever been since they betrayed Joseph. They had a ways to go yet—it was still a work in progress—but the absence of envy over Benjamin's favored treatment at the table showed that they were making progress.

> The thing they feared the most was precisely what they did not get.

And then something like freedom was beginning to displace their fears. God wanted to hang a message of freedom over their lives: freedom from a crippling past and a misshapen future.

For the thing they feared the most (this ruler arbitrarily lording it over them) was precisely what they did not get.

They came with a cringing conscience, fearing they might be made slaves and, heaven forbid, lose their flea-bitten donkeys. But instead of being enslaved, they were served as never before: with grace and love, kindness and compassion.

The message of their father was always that they were second-rate. The message of their conscience was "Be afraid. Be very afraid. If anyone finds out, you are doomed."

But the message of God is life. Life and death are in the power of the tongue, and from the tongue of God, the message is always offering life. In this text God is saying, "You matter to Me. Taste My kindness. Taste and see that the Lord is good. And I am at work to set you free, even though for now, it is still a work in progress." In what follows in the story, more work was going to be done, because God was not going to let Joseph's brothers go back to live in the basement of a status-quo life. He wanted to set them fully free.

> Life and death are in the power of the tongue, and from the tongue of God, the message is always offering life.

There is a sorrow found in Christian families when faith skips a generation. My grandmother, who I knew only very briefly, I see only now was an earnest believer. I often think that it must have been her prayers for her grandchildren, hurled into a future she would never inhabit, that landed on me and were answered in my life.

When she died, her pastor from the Caroline Street Gospel Rescue Mission, the Reverend Vern Van Duezen, conducted the service. I was about seven or eight at the time, facing the reality of death for the first time. It was a scary time for a little kid. And I remember standing at the grave-side troubled by all of it.

When the last prayers were prayed and the last words were spoken, the reverend simply put his hand on my head, smiled, and said, "God bless you, son." That's all. Then he turned and walked away with everyone who was heading back to their cars.

Now, I don't think of that moment every day. But I doubt there is a week that goes by in my Christian life when I don't think back to that day and that simple prayer and conclude that the Reverend Vern Van Duezen spoke a word that put the blessing of God upon my life in some way that might never have happened if he had never spoken that word.

I believe it was a word of blessing that held more power than he likely knew when he gave it. It was a word of more importance than he could have guessed. And maybe in some way I'll never understand, it softened my heart so that the prayers of a grandmother might have their way in me about two decades later when, as a young man, I came to faith in Christ.

The Caroline Street Gospel Rescue Mission is long closed. It was an inner-city mission in a harbor city for sailors on the Great Lakes, and time and tide passed it by. The reverend watched helplessly as it came to a struggling end along with his ministry. He never saw the kind of blessing in his work that dwelt in that simple prayer of blessing he laid upon my life that day at my grandmother's graveside.

But I like to think he is a prime stakeholder in all the blessing I have known in all my life: my marriage, my family, and my ministry all across the years. A blessing beyond measure. A blessing whose every recounting humbles me.

> Your identity is not in your mistakes or shame. Your identity is in Him.

A blessing that really began when he spoke that life-giving word over me at the edge of a grave of death. It is a word that has lingered. It has hung around. It has left its mark.

Life and death *are* in the power of the tongue. God is not in the death-speaking business. So God's word to you is not the crippled word of a weak and broken father like Jacob, who never figured out how to really love his sons. God's word to you is not the shaming word of a wounded conscience buried under a dark cloud of unspoken secrets.

No. God's word to you is that He is for you to bless you and to deliver you from yourself if need be. Your identity is not in your mistakes or shame. Your identity is in Him. He wants to hang a sign over your life that says, "You are Mine and you are loved and you are free from all of yesterday's deforming experiences."

It is as if God leans over the balcony of time to speak life to you. And as Joshua once said to God's people, "Today, I set before you life and death. Choose life" (see Deuteronomy 30:19). Could it be any clearer than that?

11

Repentance an Inch at a Time

✦ Genesis 44:1–34 ✦

In the same way, I tell you, there is joy in the presence of the angels of God over one sinner who repents.

—LUKE 15:10 NASB

It does not matter how slowly you go so long as you do not stop.

—CONFUCIUS

IF LOVING PEOPLE were easy, everyone would do it. But it's not and they don't. It's not easy to love a parent who plays favorites. It's not easy to love a sibling who is obviously more favored than you by a parent. It's not easy to forget some cruel thing that what was done to you or said about you. And it's not easy to live it all down when you're the one who did it or said it.

So much fractured family history. People drag it with them all through life, it seems. And it's not just families like Jacob's from the Bible. It's your family and mine and everyone else's in some measure.

We don't have to be told we've got unprocessed pain and history. We know it in our core. We feel it in our bones. We don't get to pick our own gene pool. We get the family we are born into. And on a lot of painful days, it's not what we would have chosen.

The hard-but-honest truth is that all of us are flawed and fallen, and it's no more evident in our lives than within family. And because we are flawed and fallen, despite our best desires and our genuine need, seldom does family life, the people in it, and the relationship we have with them, ever fully provide us with what we most deeply need.

As it was with Joseph, so it is with us. Hungers such as love and acceptance, forgiveness and honesty, support and grace, often go missing when they are most needed. We are commonly left to hunger for things and expect things from family that they just never provide.

Perhaps the hardest part of all this is that the hope for a better past will always be met by the disillusionment of reality, what really happened in those years. Could it be that it really was as vacant as you remember it? It's so disquieting to realize that the longing for all we missed growing up is really only an empty nostalgia for what was never really there.

Where do you begin to repair all that negative history? Where do you begin to renew family life and family love? And we think, *God only knows!* Well, He does. And He knows it all begins with repentance.

> The longing for all we missed growing up is really only an empty nostalgia for what was never really there.

As I wrote earlier, over the years I have come to see repentance as less of an instant response and more of a continual process that results in lasting change. Repentance is this whole of idea of turning around and going the other way. It is acknowledging in godly sorrow that I was going the wrong way and then demonstrating the honesty of that acknowledgment by going the right way.

Well, in our study of the life of Joseph, his ne'er-do-well brothers had come around to the first part of the equation to some degree, but they had a long way to go on the second part. There was more repentance work that needed to be done. If it had gotten left half finished, all it would have done was perpetuate the destructive self-loathing that comes with any kind of unresolved guilt. And you cannot generate healing love from that kind of crippled inner core.

What God was doing through Joseph was exposing the guilt of the brothers because He knows full repentance is life-giving and not life-shaming; it's transforming and not humiliating. And He knows it's the only way a broken family is ever going to be in some sense reconciled.

> Full repentance is life-giving and not life-shaming; it's transforming and not humiliating.

As I mentioned in an earlier chapter, Joseph's game is not "getting even." He's not intent upon slowly torturing his brothers in an effort to get revenge. Instead, he is digging for the gold of a slow but sure repentance. And from the text we will read in this chapter, we get to see how the brothers handled the next step in that process. Take a moment now and read it through to catch the cadence of how Joseph lead his brothers toward phase two of their repentance.

> Now Joseph gave these instructions to the steward of his house: "Fill the men's sacks with as much food as they can carry, and put each man's silver in the mouth of his sack. Then put my cup, the silver one, in the mouth of the youngest one's sack, along with the silver for his grain." And he did as Joseph said.
>
> As morning dawned, the men were sent on their way with their donkeys. They had not gone far from

the city when Joseph said to his steward, "Go after those men at once, and when you catch up with them, say to them, 'Why have you repaid good with evil? Isn't this the cup my master drinks from and also uses for divination? This is a wicked thing you have done.'"

When he caught up with them, he repeated these words to them. But they said to him, "Why does my lord say such things? Far be it from your servants to do anything like that! We even brought back to you from the land of Canaan the silver we found inside the mouths of our sacks. So why would we steal silver or gold from your master's house? If any of your servants is found to have it, he will die; and the rest of us will become my lord's slaves."

"Very well, then," he said, "let it be as you say. Whoever is found to have it will become my slave; the rest of you will be free from blame."

Each of them quickly lowered his sack to the ground and opened it. Then the steward proceeded to search, beginning with the oldest and ending with the youngest. And the cup was found in Benjamin's sack. At this, they tore their clothes. Then they all loaded their donkeys and returned to the city.

Joseph was still in the house when Judah and his brothers came in, and they threw themselves to the ground before him. Joseph said to them, "What is this you have done? Don't you know that a man like me can find things out by divination?"

"What can we say to my lord?" Judah replied. "What can we say? How can we prove our innocence? God has uncovered your servants' guilt. We are now my lord's slaves—we ourselves and the one who was found to have the cup."

But Joseph said, "Far be it from me to do such a thing! Only the man who was found to have the cup will become my slave. The rest of you, go back to your father in peace."

Then Judah went up to him and said: "Pardon your servant, my lord, let me speak a word to my lord. Do not be angry with your servant, though you are equal to Pharaoh himself. My lord asked his servants, 'Do you have a father or a brother?' And we answered, 'We have an aged father, and there is a young son born to him in his old age. His brother is dead, and he is the only one of his mother's sons left, and his father loves him.'

"Then you said to your servants, 'Bring him down to me so I can see him for myself.' And we said to my lord, 'The boy cannot leave his father; if he leaves him, his father will die.' But you told your servants, 'Unless your youngest brother comes down with you, you will not see my face again.' When we went back to your servant my father, we told him what my lord had said.

"Then our father said, 'Go back and buy a little more food.' But we said, 'We cannot go down. Only if our youngest brother is with us will we go. We cannot see the man's face unless our youngest brother is with us.'

"Your servant my father said to us, 'You know that my wife bore me two sons. One of them went away from me, and I said, "He has surely been torn to pieces." And I have not seen him since. If you take this one from me too and harm comes to him, you will bring my gray head down to the grave in misery.'

"So now, if the boy is not with us when I go back to your servant my father, and if my father, whose life is closely bound up with the boy's life, sees that the boy isn't there, he will die. Your servants will bring the gray head of our father down to the grave in sorrow. Your servant guaranteed the boy's safety to my father. I said, 'If I do not bring him back to you, I will bear the blame before you, my father, all my life!'

"Now then, please let your servant remain here as my lord's slave in place of the boy, and let the boy return with his brothers. How can I go back to my father if the boy is not with me? No! Do not let me see the misery that would come on my father." (Gen. 44:1–34)

The brothers must have felt they had escaped the worst after the end of chapter 43. What a relief! After their first experience, they had greatly feared going into their second encounter with the ruler of Egypt. Chapter 43 tells the story of their fear of prison, slavery, and of course, the loss of their donkeys! But chapter 43 ends and all their worries have come to naught. They had escaped!

Now they were back in control of their world again. They were going home with Simeon and with Benjamin and with food and supplies and also this: a great story to tell around the family fire of how they feasted with the great and mighty prime minister of Egypt. They could be pretty smug about it now. Having the symptoms of their sins relieved, they thought they'd just go back to ignoring the disease again. Back to status quo.

If the story had ended there, nothing would have changed. They would have been forever trapped in the shadows of a broken family system, living a lie, still covering their sin, still not reconciled to their father, new, debilitating consequences spilling out every day, and on and on it would go. But God simply wouldn't leave them there. And you know what? He won't leave you there either.

With the cup-in-the-sack ploy, Joseph ratcheted up the pressure on his brothers to come fully clean. Yes, in the last test, they didn't ultimately abandon Simeon. But truth be told, they were forced to come back for Simeon because the famine was so severe they had to.

But in this test, Joseph wanted to find out if they would abandon Benjamin. Or had they come to the place where their love for family would matter more to them than not having to face up to their past again?

Well, there were some good early signs in this portion of the story. One was that they didn't abandon Benjamin, even when he looked as guilty as sin, as we say. They all determined to go back to face the music even though, for all they know, Benjamin had indeed stolen the ruler's cup and put all of them at risk of prison and slavery (maybe even death) if they went back.

They also went back because Judah had made a vow ensuring Benjamin's life. The brothers joined Judah in that vow. They not only had Benjamin's back; they had Judah's back as well. They could have said, "Well, Judah, this is your problem. Go back if you want; we're going home."

But they didn't. They stood with their brother when he was putting his all on the line for the one who, much like Joseph, had been favored over them by their father. This was new territory for them, having the back of a favored son instead of abandoning him as they did Joseph.

And they went back because they knew that to go home without Benjamin really would kill their father. Their contrition, the tearing of their clothes, was legitimate. They wouldn't put their father through that again. In fact, when you read Judah's mea culpa in verse 16, you realize they were all willing to endure slavery rather than break their father's heart once more.

These were changed—*and still changing*—men. And the real telling point of their repentance was found in verse 16: "'What can we say to my lord?' Judah replied. 'What can we say? How can we prove our innocence? God has uncovered your servants' guilt. We are now my lord's slaves—we ourselves and the one who was found to have the cup.'"

There was a strange combination of innocence and guilt there. The brothers really were innocent that time. But they were not innocent men. It's like when you get a speeding ticket that you feel you really didn't deserve. But in your heart of hearts, you know you deserve about a hundred others that you didn't get.

Judah was not confessing their collective guilt for a crime he and his brothers did not commit (stealing the cup); he was confessing the guilt of a buried secret that God had diligently been at work to uncover. "God has uncovered your servants' guilt."

Generations later, Moses would warn the descendants of Reuben and Gad, two of Judah's brothers, that if they failed to obey the Lord's command to fight for their brothers, it would be sinning against the Lord, "and you may be sure that your sin will find you out" (Num. 32:23).

> There is a strange combination of innocence and guilt there. The brothers really were innocent this time. But they were not innocent men.

Judah recognized that the dilemma at hand came from God's hand. God had orchestrated all of this. And Judah finally gave up the fight. It became the last straw that broke his resolve to keep living out the lie.

Still, while repentance and reconciliation were creeping forward, they were not quite there yet. Because while all of that was unfolding, Benjamin was staring around Joseph's house, befuddled and bewildered by all he was hearing, trying to put the pieces together. He must have been wondering, *What on earth is Judah talking about?*

Benjamin had no idea what the backstory was, the story behind the story. He had no idea what his ten half brothers had done to his full brother, Joseph. Think about that. There in the midst of a circumstance that revolved around him, he had no idea what guilt and fear were turning in his brothers' stomachs.

We can only wonder if he sensed a tension he could not figure out. We've all been there at some time. Some family gathering where you keep hoping against hope that the elephant in the room will not be discovered—that dark moment of family history that has your fingerprints all over it—you hope against hope that you can make it through the day without it coming into the light. And the tension of it all is giving you a migraine.

Well, for them to have acknowledged out loud, in detail, to the ruler of Egypt, their guilt regarding Joseph, was to do so before Joseph's only full brother, Benjamin. It would be like they had said to him, "Oh, by the way, the guilt we're referring to? That was twenty-two years ago when we sold your brother, Joseph, into slavery. We shamelessly broke your father's heart and cruelly left you without your only full brother for the last two decades."

The brothers' repentance continued creeping forward as Judah made his appeal to Joseph for Benjamin's life. And while it seemed obvious, be careful not to miss this: what Joseph was listening to in verse 16 was coming from his older brother Judah. Do you remember the last speech Joseph heard from Judah's lips?

It was twenty-two years ago. Joseph was seventeen at the time. And he wasn't on a throne in Egypt, in royal robes. He was in the bottom of a dried-up cistern, in a desert, stripped of his nobleman's cloak, and tossed away by his jealous brothers. And all of his cries for mercy and compassion were ignored.

But from the bottom of the cistern, he heard a voice up above. It was the voice of his brother Judah. He was making a speech, a different kind of appeal, if you like. A cruel one. He was brokering a deal with his brothers, convincing them they ought to sell Joseph into slavery. It had been years ago, but Joseph would remember that when he needed Judah the most, Judah sold him out.

Twenty-two years later, Judah was down on his knees before Joseph, trying to keep Benjamin, his father's other favorite son, out of slavery. And not just that. In an irony to beat all ironies, in offering himself as a substitute for Benjamin, Judah was offering himself as a slave to Joseph, the one he sold into slavery.

What would you be thinking about what you were hearing from Judah if you were Joseph? How much grace would it take not to lord it over your brother . . . or your sister . . . or your parents . . . or your in-laws?

Ah . . . now a shift has occurred in our thoughts. It's no longer Judah and Joseph, is it? It's you and me and the cast of characters from our messed-up family history. And across the screens of our imaginations we see the scenes played out again of all the slights and wounds we have suffered in family life across all the years. What will we do when circumstances are reversed and we have all the power and leverage?

There are certain moments when I watch TV that I have to get up and leave the room. My Marilyn is the queen of the murder mystery. And often, to build the tension of the plot, the actors show you the crime being committed . . . and for me at times, it is just too explicit. The thing I cannot bear to watch is someone being held against her will, restrained, and rendered helplessly vulnerable, and then having her will violated.

> What will we do when circumstances are reversed and we have all the power and leverage?

It took me years to figure out why my spirit reacted so strongly to such scenes. Then I remembered as a boy being pinned down by an older kid in the neighborhood, a bully. He'd pin my arms behind my head. I would be completely unable to get free.

Then he would taunt me for his amusement, sometimes spitting on me, always finding ways to leave me humiliated. So when I see a similar motif on TV, someone helplessly restrained, I have to leave the room. It's just too visceral and disturbing for me.

But I also remember years later, after I had become a Christian, when that older kid went to prison. His family abandoned him. They were too ashamed, it seemed, as if they had been humiliated by him. I think they thought they were punishing him by staying away.

From the old neighborhood, I was the only one I knew who went to visit him. It was just something God led me to do. And when I saw him, I remembered thinking how helpless I used to feel when he overpowered me and had me pinned down against my will.

And then I thought how helpless he looked in there. Trapped. Restrained. Held against his will. And I almost felt smug about it, but God wouldn't allow my heart to go there. I held all the cards of power, as it were, but in truth, all I could feel was sorrow for him

So tell me, "Joseph," what will you do with your "Judah"? Enslave him or forgive him? Offer healing grace or shaming guilt? One choice gives life, and the other traffics only in the death of all the dreams and hopes you have or once had for family life. We know what Joseph did. What will you do?

Listen to your Judah plead his case. Scores of well-known Bible scholars, folks such as F. B. Meyer, James Boice, and Henry Leopold, said there is no speech anywhere more full of pathos than this one. Boice compared it to Socrates's death eulogy by Plato for its emotive power. Donald Grey Barnhouse called it the most moving address in all the Word of God. And we can see why.

There were many powerful moments in Judah's impassioned speech. Joseph heard for the first time of his father's response to his own abduction and that Jacob still mourned for him. He heard how the further loss of Benjamin would kill his father. He learned of Judah's vow and his unshakeable commitment to keep it, even at the expense of himself. And he discovered how Judah could not bear to watch the suffering and misery his father would endure over the loss of his beloved Benjamin.

You know, if you listen closely to Judah interceding for mercy on his brother, you can almost hear the Lion of Judah interceding for us in John 17. But then, in mid-appeal. he reverted right back to the not-so-good Judah. He lied. Twice. He told this ruler of Egypt that their brother Joseph was dead and then later, perpetuated the lie, the family myth, that he was torn to pieces by a ravenous animal.

How could he do that? How could he so nobly defend his brother's life and at the same time present this mixture of truth and half-truth? And he doesn't know that it was Joseph who was sitting there listening to him bend the truth into a pretzel nobody would ever eat! How could he offer himself in self-giving love and lie while doing it?

> How could [Judah] offer himself in self-giving love and lie while doing it? . . . He was living out of his contradictions.

Because his repentance was not full and complete, he was still trying to save some face, especially in front of Benjamin, who hadn't got the whole family story. And Judah was still trying not to have to move to the place of complete vulnerability. He was afraid of what would happen if he was totally honest and straightforward.

He was living out of his contradictions . . . just like we do. On one hand you're a loving husband, and on the other you're that lazy guy who won't get off the couch to help with dishes. You're a faithful son, but you lie to your mother about how you feel about your sister.

We are complex and conflicted at so many levels. We often find ourselves living a contradiction between what we claim to be and what we really are. It's not hypocrisy. But it's some kind of cousin. And it's who we are on a lot of days.

The good news in Joseph's response of love is that we learn that God's love is not conditioned by our contradictions. Joseph loved his brothers across all the history he had with them and with all of their flaws. We see pictured here what unconditional love looks like. And we see it in more ways than one.

My friend Dr. Steve Seamands, who teaches at Asbury Theological Seminary, sent me a quote from a book by an Old Testament scholar named Robert Alter. As Alter studied this encounter between Joseph and Judah, he observed the newfound, remarkable love of Judah for his father, Jacob, a love despite all his father's sins and failures and inadequacies as a dad. The Judah who cruelly wounded his father and let him suffer that wound by believing a lie for more than two decades, can no longer bear the thought of seeing his father suffer.

> God's love is not conditioned by our contradictions. In Joseph's story we see what unconditional love looks like.

Alter pointed out that even in his speech, Judah acknowledged that Jacob loved Joseph and Benjamin more than the rest and that even then, Jacob's life was totally bound up in the life of the boy. He wrote:

> A basic biblical perception about . . . human relations . . . is that love is unpredictable, arbitrary, at times perhaps seemingly unjust, and Judah now comes to an acceptance of that fact with all its consequences. His father, he states clearly to Joseph, has singled out Benjamin for a special love, as he singled out Rachel's other son before. It is a painful reality of favoritism with which Judah, in contrast to the earlier jealousy over Joseph, is here reconciled, out of filial duty [as a son] and more, out of filial love. His entire speech is motivated by the deepest empathy for his father, by a real understanding of what it means for the old man's very life to be bound up with that of the lad.[1]

My friend Steve reflected on this and concluded that what Judah did was to finally love and accept his father for who he was. Even though Jacob hadn't changed—he was still playing favorites—Judah was reconciled to that and accepted him and loved him for who he was. He knew Jacob would probably never change, but that was okay; he loved him nonetheless.

Then Steve had this great thought: "This is a profound message for all of us, I think, of what it means to finally be reconciled to the faults and sins and failures of our parents; knowing that we may never get from them what we long for and deserve, but loving and accepting them for who they are nonetheless."[2]

We must learn to love and accept people whose lives are made complex with all of *their* contradictions, as much as we want people to love and accept us when we live out of *our* contradictions. Some folks may never change and become who we want them to be or need them to be. But our task is not to change people. Our task, ultimately, is to love them and let God do the work of changing, as He did here with Joseph's brothers.

And do remember that it cuts back in the other direction as well, as we see in Judah with all of his blind spots. Unconditional love and forgiveness and acceptance are not just about Judahs loving Jacobs: it's about us Josephs loving the Judahs in all of *their* contradictions.

It is loving and accepting and forgiving the noble son pleading for his brother's life while he lies doing it.

It is parents loving their kids who lie to them about everything from cleaning their rooms to doing their homework to their sexual conduct.

It is siblings loving and forgiving one another when everyone knows what went down but no one can seem to bring it up.

And can I be honest at this point and admit that on a lot of days there is more of Judah in me than there is Joseph? God is commonly showing me where I don't live into all I was called to be in Jesus. He has the Holy Spirit take a highlighter to my contradictions on a daily basis. And can I be even more honest? I don't think I'm alone in that.

As we become aware of our own contradictions, our hearts blush. But that's a good thing. It keeps us from the stench of self-righteousness, the ugly pretense that we are the only holy ones left. A blushing heart is really a kindness from God showing He is still at work in us; His spirit has not given up on us. He is determined to lead us to repentance, shaping us into Christlikeness and renewing the relationships that matter so much to us.

> A blushing heart is really a kindness from God showing He is still at work in us.

I don't know what Joseph expected for an outcome when he devised this plot with the cup. But whatever he had hoped for was certainly met and matched by the response of Judah and his brothers. I don't know what I expected when I visited that neighbor kid in prison, but I do know that we are able to talk, friend with friend, and the ground between us is no longer uneven.

And I don't know what you will expect if you offer a way back into relationship for those who are estranged in your family's life or your friendship networks. But I do know that God has a stake in those lives. And His stake is to bless and to heal and to reconcile.

Is There Any Chance for a Better Tomorrow?

"Forgive us our trespasses as we forgive those who trespass against us."

—MATTHEW 6:12, FROM THE CATECHISM
OF THE CATHOLIC CHURCH

"Anyhow, the breach between them widened. Their division [over an opinion] only gave the two sides a high-toned language that kept the differences raw. Time, which is supposed to heal, [instead] only made them old."

—WENDELL BERRY IN *JAYBER CROW*

I HAD AN old friend who, for reasons real or imagined and which no longer even matter, turned away from me in anger long ago and didn't speak to me for almost twenty years. Then something changed. His wife got terminal cancer. Not long ago, my Marilyn and I drove thirty-two hundred miles over five days to attend the funeral of his wife, to be of comfort to him. With sincere tears in his eyes, he told me it meant the world to him that we did.

Now, how can that be? What changed? What makes that kind of relationship transformation possible? Because in the real world, that's not possible. The traffic of guilt in relationships runs down both sides of that street, and the accidents are numerous and commonly fatal. Have you been run off the road lately? Then you know how real life works.

We've come to a pause in our story between the self-evident guilt of the brothers at the end of Genesis 44 and Joseph's need to do something about that guilt in Genesis 45. Would he be like his father, Jacob, with Reuben and ignore it, hoping it will all go away? Would he be like his brothers and prolong their pain as they did his?

A more spiritually mature Joseph realized that if they were to have any chance of a tomorrow as a family, it would all depend on his ability to heroically forgive them. It had to be heroic because their betrayal was so epic. Don't assume that the luxuries of Egypt and the good life he'd come to know had assuaged the pain of what his brothers did to him.

Even when we have moved long past the hurts we experienced earlier in life into fuller and richer lives, we think we are over them, but don't be fooled. Just let a face or a moment come up on the screen of our imagination and the pain of it walks right back in the front door of our hearts. Ask the spouse cruelly hurt in a divorce if he or she has forgotten. Ask the child abused by an adult. Ask the betrayed friend. Can they just forget and move on now that the past is in the past and the present is brighter? We've already learned that Joseph has moved on, but he certainly didn't forget. But can he forgive?

Can we talk about forgiveness? The comedian Lily Tomlin was quoted in *The Week* magazine. She said, "Forgiveness means giving up all hope for a better past."[1] There is some truth to that. There is an acknowledgment in her statement that the past is littered with pain. It's full of regrettable moments and experiences that cause the human memory to wince.

But there is also something wrong with her statement. There is a tone of hopeless resignation to it, suggesting that we only seek forgiveness when we cannot spin the past or deconstruct it to fit our version of it. When we cannot find a way to remake yesterday to suit us, we are forced to do something about it. Yet what we most commonly do is call it no big deal when it is. Call it water under the bridge when it's not. In doing so we heal the sins of the people lightly (cf. Jer. 6:14 RSV) and carry the offense in our hearts as ammunition for the battle that inevitably comes later.

The culturally cheap variety of forgiveness is a faux forgiveness that simply cannot handle the past honestly. As Wendell Berry said, "Time, which is supposed to heal, [instead] only made them old."[2] If you've lived in this world long enough, you know that only genuine, Christian forgiveness enables life to move forward into anything that resembles relational health and wellness. It's the only thing that gives tomorrow a chance to be a place you'd want to live in and a future you'd want to live with.

> The culturally cheap variety of forgiveness is faux forgiveness that simply cannot handle the past.

Again, if you've lived in this world long enough, you know how bad we are at doing the work of forgiveness. Because of this, the tomorrows and futures we are commonly walking into are made uninviting to say the least and tragic to say the most. Guilt and shame bleed all over life every day and everywhere. The hard truth be told, no one seems that motivated to stop the bleeding.

Why? Because that is where, to our sorrow and in our fallenness, we commonly like to leave the people who have hurt us: bruised, bleeding, and ashamed. It doesn't matter what they did to us. In fact, *the offense we are least likely to forgive in others is often the one we are most likely to commit ourselves*. But no matter: if I can leave you in shame and guilt, I win, right?

Having walked through much of Joseph's life story, you might begin to understand in a fuller way why he is often noted as the most Christlike figure in the Old Testament. The power was all his to condemn and reject his brothers. He held all the cards but refused to play them. And us? On a lot of days we're reaching for the ace up our sleeves, trying to trump the ones who've hurt us.

Could it be true that when all is said and done, we really don't want to forgive? We've got scores we want to settle, and vengeance has a cold but common taste in our mouths that somehow we find appetizing. Our fallen inclination is not to forgive.

It's much like what Rebekah said to Jacob in Genesis 27, in the Bible's best summary of every sibling rivalry ever known. Do you remember it? After Jacob had cheated Esau out of his inheritance, Rebekah told Jacob: "Behold your brother Esau is consoling himself concerning you by planning to kill you" (v. 42 NASB). Who is it that owes you one? Who stole your moment or took your place who now needs to make it up to you? In your heart of hearts, do you really want the best for your Jacob?

If real human experience is to be trusted, then it seems *we most often want the people who have hurt us to feel guilty for doing so.* We want them to feel what we felt: belittled or ashamed. We want them to feel the pain of our woundedness. In candor, we want to do it in such a way that they know we hold the moral high ground and that they are forever beholden to us.

Is it any wonder, then, that so many of the relationships in life we experience are so dysfunctional and broken? How can you build or rebuild any kind of sensible, loving relationship on that kind of uneven ground? As in the popular Broadway play *Doubt*, have you ever tried picking up a pillow full of feathers after they've all been thrown to the wind?

Take the line in the Lord's Prayer as it was taught to many of us as children: "And forgive us our trespasses as we forgive those who trespass against us." It assumes a lot, doesn't it? It assumes that we regularly forgive those who sin against us. It assumes that we live out of this disposition to forgive, that of course God will forgive us because we are living and moving and breathing in this constant stream of forgiving people all the time.

But are we? Your father or your mother: any need for forgiveness to be applied there? Your adult children and your not-so-adult children who think they are adults: any lack of forgiveness there? Wounds within the wider family: got any? Is there real peace around the family table, or is there an elephant in the room that no one wants to talk about?

Because until that elephant is dead, there is no real hope for a renewal of the family relationship. Maybe that's why funerals can seem to bring out the worst in people, why the tensions are often so great. Could it be that when the time was available to do the work of forgiveness, it did not get done? I think many of us (or all of us!) have found too many funerals crowded by the elephants of unforgiveness in the room.

> Funerals seem to bring out the worst in people because when the time was available to do the work of forgiveness, it did not get done.

Make no mistake about it: forgiving is not easy work. A brooding grudge becomes a part of our identity, and who wants to give up a piece of ourselves? There is also the fear of the inequity it creates; the feeling that you are exposed and vulnerable now and can be taken advantage of all over again because you let those who hurt you off the hook of their well-deserved guilt. Forgiveness pushes us out to the very edges of our capacity to love, and more often than not, we don't want to go there or make the effort.

Nor is forgiveness cheap. Every time we come to the sacrament of communion, we are reminded of the cost. In forgiveness, God does not wink at sin as if it's no big deal, as if it's water under the bridge. The death of His Son reminds us that to hurt, betray, or offend someone is a big deal. God knows sin hurts. And we know that forgiveness does not replace the requirement of justice. Justice was served at Calvary. It is forgiveness that adds divine value to the justice satisfied there.

For pure justice to be served, for the Son of God to forgive us our sins, the price had to be paid somehow, someway. Jesus made the effort, pushing Himself out to the farthest edges of His love. He paid the price Himself: at Calvary. *Pure love paid the price of pure justice so that by pure grace we might be forever forgiven.* The question Matthew 6:12 begs is, do we have any such pure love for the people who currently stand outside of our measure of grace? I told you it was costly.

There was a price to pay, and Jesus paid it. Will you and I pay it? There is a Chinese proverb that says, "The beginning of wisdom is to call a thing what it really is." The costly price of forgiveness is always paid in the currency of pride. Frederick Buechner wrote that to forgive somebody is to say, one way or another,

> You have done something mean spirited and cruel to me, and by all rights, I should just call it quits between us. My pride and self respect demand nothing less.
>
> However, though I make no guarantee I will ever forget what you did, and though we both may carry the scars for life, I refuse to let it stand between us. I still want you for my friend.[3]

There is no denial of reality in any of this. Someone has treated you as less than a person. You have been wounded terribly, and you didn't deserve it. But in forgiveness you determine that you won't let your wounded pride forever define the character of that relationship.

In forgiveness, especially within family life, you eat the pain of it, and because the wounding never seems to end, who wants a steady diet of pain? You absorb the hurt and pay the cost of surrendered pride to keep that relationship alive. You ask God for the grace to love that person as you once did, much as you ask Him for that same grace to keep loving you each time you go back to Him after wounding Him. All of that lives in those expensive three little words, "I forgive you."

The play *Doubt* portrayed it well. You and I can never regather all the feathers in the pillow any more than we can unscramble an egg. The only thing that changes the past between two people is forgiveness of a divine quality.

The love of God poured into your heart and mine by God's grace alone is the only resource that can make such divine forgiveness possible. The enabling power to forgive is Him loving me and His love within me loving you. I can forgive you without losing face because it is His face that matters most.

> In forgiveness you determine that you won't let your wounded pride forever define the character of that relationship.

I remember years ago reading a telling comment by the much-decorated U.S. Olympic diver Greg Louganis. He was asked where he got the courage to risk so greatly, knowing his critics awaited the opportunity to record each flaw. And he said something like, "Even if I blow this dive, my mother will still love me." Secure in that love, he could risk anything. Secure in our Father's love, we can risk forgiving, though the relational dangers are inherent and self-evident. Ever dive off the high tower? Then you know the risk forgiving takes.

Still, curiously, there is a price to be paid in accepting forgiveness as well. For if I accept the forgiveness offered me, it must mean that I truly needed to be forgiven: that I really was mean-spirited or cruel, that I was less than what

God meant me to be. It must mean I was, in fact, unloving, which is to be unlike Jesus, unlike a Christian. I was, in fact, ungodly. In receiving and accepting forgiveness, that is what I acknowledge as true.

It seems, then, that the great price of forgiving is paid in pride on both sides. The one who forgives swallows her wounded pride in order to forgive. The one who accepts forgiveness swallows her humbled pride in order to be forgiven. In realizing this we discover that the elephant in the room at the family gathering that needs to be put to death is actually pride. Nakedly put, raw human pride, carnal and fallen, is the thing that always stands in the way of forgiveness. No wonder C. S. Lewis, in his book *Mere Christianity*, identified pride as the greatest sin of all. It kills all that is good in life.

> If I accept the forgiveness offered me, it must mean that I truly needed to be forgiven.

But as we move from shadows to light, we discover that the great reward of forgiveness is freedom. When someone you have hurt forgives you, you have just kept yourself from the life-crippling distortions that come from a guilty conscience. If Jacob had forgiven Reuben, he would not have spent decades disfigured by his guilt and shame. When we are forgiven, the guilt is gone along with all the attendant baggage of regret and shame. When you forgive someone who has wronged you, you are spared the corrosive pain of the spiritual cancer of bitterness. The bitter root never gets planted. For both parties, forgiveness brings the freedom to be at peace inside your own skin and gladness to be in each other's presence.

We have learned two things: the great and costly price of forgiveness is always pride, and yet forgiveness is the only way to real, relational freedom. Then, as you might expect, the price of pride can only be paid in the coinage of humility. Perhaps that is why Paul wrote in Philippians 2:3–8:

Do nothing out of selfish ambition or vain conceit. Rather, in humility value others above yourselves, not looking to your own interests but each of you to the interests of the others. In your relationships with one another, have the same mindset as Christ Jesus: Who, being in very nature God, did not consider equality with God something to be used to his own advantage; rather, he made himself nothing by taking the very nature of a servant, being made in human likeness. And being found in appearance as a man, he humbled himself by becoming obedient to death— even death on a cross!

I have often wondered—perhaps you have as well—what needs to die in me in order that I might forgive someone and move on with life, What needs to be nailed to a cross in humility so that life can be what it's meant to be? It may have many faces, but its name is always the same, isn't it? It's pride.

I wonder how many of us parents need to humble ourselves before our children, and ask forgiveness from them. It works back the other way too, doesn't it? Children and adult children who need to ask forgiveness of their parents. Maybe all of us should remember that if Jesus humbled Himself on a cross before us, we could humble ourselves before our parents or our kids or even our siblings.

> When it comes to forgiveness in family life, we like to count up the offenses and make sure we are not owed one.

Do you remember that conversation in Matthew 18 between Peter and Jesus when Peter was trying to get a handle on how much forgiving was required to be considered a righteous person, a person rightly related to God and to others? Peter thought forgiving seven times was being pretty generous. Then Jesus came back and said to try seventy times seven (KJV). In other words, stop counting.

But that is our problem in family life. We like to count. The interfering. The controlling behaviors. The criticisms and comparisons. When it comes to forgiveness in family life, we like to count up the offenses and make sure we are not owed one. We don't realize we're trying to count the feathers in a pillow. But it feeds an appetite in us: that black-hole appetite for revenge. We keep a ledger in our hearts of every slight we have ever suffered from mothers or fathers, sisters or brothers, then on to friends and enemies, bosses and coworkers, neighbors and whatever. Finally, we say in our hearts, *Okay, that's it. Your number's up. I'm stopping the forgiveness I've been offering.*

In Peter's day, seven was a culturally perfect number. In Hebrew, it is related to the idea of wholeness. When Peter suggested seven, he figured that he was being generous in forgiving beyond all expectation. When Jesus answered him with seventy times seven, if you listen closely to your Bible, you can actually hear the wind going out of Peter's sails.

Jesus' use of this expression is really a common Hebrew idiom that means times beyond counting. It is sort of like your mother saying, "If I've told you once, I've told you a million times." Christ is saying that Christian righteousness demands that we forgive without keeping record of the number of times forgiveness has been sought and granted.

> Forgiveness does not require you to keep opening your heart to ongoing exposure to an abusive relationship.

Where would Jesus get an idea like that? Simple, really. He got it from His father and how He forgives us: times beyond number and often for the same offenses over and over and over again. Including all the times we have needed forgiveness for being unforgiving.

Yet let me add this: Forgiveness does not require you to keep opening your heart to ongoing exposure to an abusive relationship. You may remember that David forgave Saul for trying to kill him. Yet he never went back to the palace for Saul to throw more spears at him. He forgave him but did not entrust his heart to him.

If you have someone in your life who specializes in throwing spears, your place is to forgive that person. But you are not obligated to keep exposing yourself to his or her abuses. Forgiveness makes a future possible. Yet it does not mean you have to entrust your heart to that individual.

To whom much is given, much will be required. Because we have been forgiven much, we must forgive. It is seldom as dramatic as the newspaper stories of parents forgiving a drunk driver or a rape victim forgiving her perpetrator. Besides, as I said earlier, forgiveness does not replace the need for justice in such cases. Even when the offender is forgiven by the victim, he or she is still required to go to jail.

The much-required part of forgiveness is most often in family life. Those times when we are called to forgive the look of disfavor we got across the room. Forgive that tone of voice that speaks only condemnation upon us. Forgive the thanklessness of family, that feeling of being used. Forgive being overlooked, passed by, cold-shouldered, not honored, not chosen, not esteemed by those whose esteem we long for most.

Do you remember the parable of the unforgiving servant in Matthew 18, who, when all was said and done, did not forgive the one indebted to him? He ended up bound in an inescapable prison, trying to pay back what could not be repaid in a hundred lifetimes—a prison where life for him was torture until the day he died.

He is as one of those people we meet at those funerals I wrote about earlier. Prisoners all. They are the people everyone wants to avoid. They are full of complaint and resentment and bitterness. They are toxic to be around. How did they get that way?

They were the proud, unforgiving people who counted every offense and are still looking to have justice prove them right for counting so well. Write this down: justice without forgiveness is just hell on earth for the human soul. Thus they have lived in a prison cell of bitterness built by their own unforgiving choices.

I used to think that the most common emotion at a funeral was grief. Then, as years passed, I thought it was guilt. Now I think I have learned that it's regret. I hear it behind so many spoken and unspoken words. I see it behind the eyes that have lost the ability to cry. Regret. All the things that could have been and never were because there was too much counting of offenses going on.

At the funeral of my old friend's wife, what surprised me was how both of us were so comfortable in our own skin and in each other's presence. There was no shame or guilt, no regret or bitterness. By the grace of God, genuine forgiveness had dismantled all the barriers so that both of us could be touched by the comfort of human love and honest sympathy, all because along the journey, the costly work of forgiveness got done. That work left only a freedom in each other's presence that only the love and grace of God could account for. We were simply at home with each other.

Yet there was an unnecessary sorrow present that had no place there. There was an elephant in the room . . . a legacy within my friend's wider family. It chilled the room and froze out a healing love that was deeply needed. It limited the many conversations that should have been had that just never happened. Tragically, the elephant was completely unresponsive when my old friend was so humbly holding out grace and love to all those who had fed that elephant for years.

We all know people and families like this. Yet have we ever stopped to consider that it might be us, might be me, might be our family? Are there elephants that have to be dealt with while the time is still available to do so? If you are reading this, there may very well still be time.

I do know this: forgiveness offers the chance at the grace of honest reconciliation, an opportunity at life together rather than death together. I felt it in the embrace my old friend gave me when it seemed he would never let go. I saw it in his eyes and read it in his tears.

While forgiveness never forgets the past, it is no longer trapped by it, held in bondage to it. I heard that in my friend's voice on the phone just a few weeks later as we talked about the events of those days and what the future held for us as friends. For us forgiveness has opened up a wider and fuller future.

> Forgiveness offers an opportunity at life together rather than death together.

It's spring here this morning, and the promise of life is everywhere. I see it on the trees in my yard. They are like old friends to me. Well, actually they are like old family, really, because they are.

I have a tree on my front lawn named Florence. I have another named Tina and another named Vince. My Marilyn and I planted them as we lost parents: memorials to lives that were meant to be remembered, even for all their raggedness.

Recently my old friend and I planted a tree in my yard named in honor of his wife. This morning I looked out on her and thought to myself, *Isn't it life-giving when forgiveness does its work?*

Then I thought, *I think I'll give my old friend a call and ask him how he is doing.*

Notes

Acknowledgments

1. Vance Havner, *Pepper 'n' Salt* (Old Tappan, NJ: Revell, 1966), 59.

Chapter 1: Negatives Found in the Family Album

1. Barbara Brown Taylor, *The Preaching Life* (Lanham, MD: Rowman & Littlefield, 1993), 59–60; emphasis added.
2. Thomas Lynch, *The Undertaking: Life Studies from the Dismal Trade* (New York: W. W. Norton, 1997), 53.

Chapter 2: When Dreams Become Nightmares

1. J. K. Rowling, *Harry Potter and the Chamber of Secrets* (New York: Scholastic, 2000), 333.
2. Jeff Kluger, *The Sibling Effect: What the Bonds Among Brothers and Sisters Reveal Among Us* (New York: Penguin, 2011) n.p.
3. Ibid.

Chapter 3: The Soap-Opera Life

1. Don J. Snyder, *Of Time and Memory: My Parents' Love Story* (New York: Alfred A. Knopf, 1999), 5.
2. Wendell Berry, *Jayber Crow: A Novel* (Washington, DC: Counterpoint, 2000), 12.
3. Geoffrey Chaucer, *The Canterbury Tales*, new ed. (Oxford: Oxford University Press, 1998), 439.
4. Frederick Buechner, *Telling Secrets: A Memoir*, repr. ed (San Francisco: HarperOne, 2000), 33.
5. Barbara Brown Taylor, *The Preaching Life* (Lanham, MD: Rowman & Littlefield, 1993), 51.
6. François Fénelon, *The Seeking Heart* (Sargent, GA: SeedSowers, 1992), 133.

Chapter 4: All the Right Choices, All the Wrong Results

1. Kilian McDonnell, *Swift, Lord, You Are Not* (Collegeville, MN: The Order of Saint Benedict, 2003), 32.
2. Adapted from William Congreve, *The Mourning Bride*, act 3, scene 1.

Chapter 6: When God Falls Silent

1. Emily Dickinson, "A Great Hope Fell," in *The Poems of Emily Dickinson*, Reading Ed., ed. R. W. Franklin (Cambridge and London: Belknap Press, 1999), 472.
2. François Fénelon, *Talking with God*, Contemporary English ed., eds. Hal M. Helms and Robert J. Edmonson (Brewster, MA: Paraclete Press, 2009), chap. 11.

Chapter 7: The Man Could Do No Wrong

1. Dietrich Bonhoeffer, *Letters and Papers from Prison*, ed. Eberhard Bethge, enl. ed. (New York: Touchstone, 1997).

Chapter 8: The Not-So-Glad Reunion

1. William Shakespeare, *Hamlet*, act 3, scene 1.

Chapter 9: Are You Sure You Want Alone Time with God?

1. H. L. Mencken, ed. and annot., *A Mencken Chrestomathy* (New York: Knopf Doubleday, 2012), 617.
2. James Montgomery Boice, *Genesis: An Expositional Commentary*, vol. 3: *Genesis 37:1–50:26* (Grand Rapids, MI: Zondervan, 1987).

Chapter 10: The Message Hanging over Your Life

1. Rick Pitino once said this in a press conference when he was confronted about a sexual liaison he had with a woman at a restaurant.

Chapter 11: Repentance an Inch at a Time

1. Robert Alter, *The Art of Biblical Narrative*, 2nd ed. (New York: Basic Books, 2011), 217–18.
2. This was sent to me in an e-mail communication from Dr. Steve Seamands, who was a member of my congregation at the time, and we were interacting around the story of Joseph.

Chapter 12: Is There Any Chance for a Better Tomorrow?

1. "Wit and Wisdom" column, *The Week*, February 10, 2011.
2. Wendell Berry, *Jayber Crow: A Novel* (Washington, DC: Counterpoint, 2000), 204.
3. Frederick Buechner, *Wishful Thinking* (New York: HarperCollins, 1993), 32–33.